The New
MRS LEE'S
COOKBOOK
Vol. 2

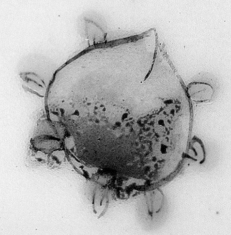

The New MRS LEE'S COOKBOOK

Vol. 2

Straits Heritage Cuisine

Foreword by **Minister Mentor Lee Kuan Yew**
Written by **Mrs Lee Chin Koon**
Updated by her granddaughter **Shermay Lee**

TIMES EDITIONS

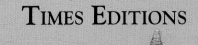

Food Preparation: Shermay Lee
Managing Editor: Jamilah Mohd Hassan
Editor: Lydia Leong
Designer: Ang Lee Ming
Photographer: Yu Hui Ying
Photographer (Portrait): Steve Loh
Production Co-ordinator: Nor Sidah Haron

Published by Times Editions – Marshall Cavendish
An imprint of Marshall Cavendish International (Asia) Private Limited
A member of Times Publishing Limited
Times Centre, 1 New Industrial Road, Singapore 536196
Tel: (65) 6213 9288   Fax: (65) 6285 4871
E-mail: te@sg.marshallcavendish.com
Online Bookstore: http://www.timesone.com.sg/te

Malaysian Office:
Federal Publications Sdn Berhad (General & Reference Publishing) (3024-D)
Times Subang, Lot 46, Persiaran Teknologi Subang
Subang Hi-Tech Industrial Park
Batu Tiga, 40000 Shah Alam
Selangor Darul Ehsan, Malaysia
Tel: (603) 5635 2191   Fax: (603) 5635 2706
E-mail: cchong@tpg.com.my

National Library Board (Singapore) Cataloguing in Publication Data

Lee, Chin Koon,- Mrs.
The new Mrs Lee's cookbook. Vol. 2, Straits heritage cuisine /- written by Mrs Lee Chin Koon ;
updated by Shermay Lee. – Singapore :- Times Editions,- c2004.
p. cm.
ISBN : 981-232-705-3
ISBN : 981-232-953-6 (pbk.)

1.Cookery, Singapore. I. Lee, Shermay,- 1975- II. Title.
TX724.5.S
641.595957 – dc21   SLS2004026579

Printed in Singapore by Tien Wah Press (Pte) Ltd

Contents

Foreword

*Senior Minister
Singapore*

My mother loved good food and liked to cook for her children. When I went to college and had to eat institutional food in the hall, I was miserable.

After I married and set up home, we had Cantonese maids. They were good cooks, but they could not quite reproduce the Peranakan dishes my mother cooked. So we got used to different standards.

A year ago, my niece, Shermay Lee, updated my mother's cookbook and called it *The New Mrs Lee's Cookbook Vol. 1: Nonya Cuisine.* It won an international award.

She has invited me to dinner at her cooking school in Chip Bee Gardens. Her dishes evoked memories of my mother's food. But either because with age my palate has become dulled and jaded, or the ingredients are no longer the same; in my memory, my mother's dishes were better. However, for those who have never tasted my mother's cooking, Shermay's will be the next best available.

Lee Kuan Yew
3 August 2004

Introduction

*Thanks be to God whose blessings are more than
I could have asked for or imagined.*

The overwhelming success of *The New Mrs Lee's Cookbook Vol. 1: Nonya Cuisine* exceeded my expectations by every measure.

Relaunching my late grandmother's recipes was something I did with great enthusiasm but also with a sense of responsibility because of the culinary significance of her famous orange-coloured cookbook. The overall concept of the revised cookbooks is a result of very deliberate choices that my publisher and I made to update and modernise her cookbook without losing its credibility and authenticity. We set out to revamp the layout yet make minimal changes to the recipes, except where absolutely necessary, and to enhance it with photographs that detail the texture and colour of each dish.

I added special touches to the first of the revised cookbooks, such as making subtle historic references to the original cookbook. I was encouraged to hear from readers who appreciated these extra efforts. These included the special request I made to Dr Wee Kim Wee to write a new Foreword since he had written the Foreword for my grandmother's cookbook some 30 years ago, as well as the use of the same seasoned *kuali* (wok) and *batu lesung* (mortar and pestle) that my grandmother had used in her original cookbook, to illustrate the Basic Kitchen Equipment section. Small details like these may generally go unnoticed but are nevertheless there to add that special touch.

Even more rewarding is the fact that several people told me the cookbook had renewed their interest in Nonya cooking, and many dishes are now re-appearing on their dining tables once again. A few ladies whose mothers learnt cooking from my grandmother are also now attending my classes two generations later.

The New Mrs Lee's Cookbook Vol. 1: Nonya Cuisine is a collection of the classic Nonya recipes my grandmother mastered when she was young, as she was taught the rudiments of cooking by my great grandmother in preparation for marriage. She later continued to cook these perennial favourites, such as Ayam Buah Keluak, Garam Asam and Mee Siam, as a mother of five, and then as a grandmother of seventeen.

This second volume, *The New Mrs Lee's Cookbook Vol. 2: Straits Heritage Cuisine*, reflects a later phase in her life particularly from the 1950s to the 1970s. Although the recipes appear very diverse, they testify to her great love of cooking and her ability to embrace new ideas. My mother, the editor of the original cookbook, describes my grandmother as an adventurous and passionate cook who often managed to befriend other chefs, many from famous restaurants, to learn new cooking techniques and recipes.

Included in this second volume are a number of Cantonese dishes which my grandmother learnt from Chef Tham Yui Kai. It is likely that she learnt from him such dishes as Sook Muy Tong, Chow Har, Foo Yong Hai, Chicken Filling in a Yam Basket, Chicken and Cashew Nuts, Chicken Wrapped in Paper, Sweet and Sour Pork, Yok Lan Gai and Minute Steak, to name a few. She later learnt how to make dim sum from another chef, although we have no written record of those recipes.

She also used to fill her time teaching cooking to expatriate wives, including wives of the diplomatic corps, in particular, wives of British and Australian military officers. She taught them Curry Tiffin, the simplified version of local dishes such as Satay and Sayur Lodeh, and other home-style Chinese favourites, often altering the recipes to take into account the availability of ingredients in their native homes as well as to suit their palates.

In addition, there are a few recipes that must have emerged from the kitchens of Hainanese 'cookboys' in colonial homes or country clubs. These recipes include Boneless Stuffed Chicken, Pork Chops and Chicken Stew. The use of light soy sauce and ginger

Special thanks to my aunt Monica for the use of this photograph which even now sits in her living room. It captures my grandmother in the best way I remember her: industrious, animated and happy in her kitchen. I believe the dish before her is Nasi Kuning which is included in this cookbook. She was teaching it at a cooking class held in her home.

juice combined with Worcestershire sauce and butter reflect the fusion of East and West before it became fashionable—this is what I like to call 'old school' fusion.

Her mother-in-law had lived in Indonesia and brought quite a few Indonesian recipes to the family dining table, so there was also Indonesian-Dutch influence in her cooking, for instance, the dish Rissoles.

Then there are other popular recipes such as Roti Jala, Mutton Curry and Curry Devil, which reflect the Malay, Indian and Eurasian influences in Singapore and would best be categorised as 'street' or 'hawker' food.

My grandmother's recipes, like other family heirloom recipes, are tried-and-tested and continue to be our family favourites. It is, in a sense, our 'comfort' food, as these are dishes that we grew up with.

More significantly, I have increasingly begun to treasure the heritage of her cooking with the passing years. The knowledge culminated in her recipes are like a snapshot of a Nonya woman's life during the early days of Singapore, and reflect a segment of Singapore's culinary heritage. It would be a great pity if the innovation and skill it took to create and refine these recipes are not preserved for future generations and showcased beyond the shores of Singapore.

I strive as best I can, to reproduce and revive these dishes. But I know it is difficult to perfectly replicate them, although I may come very close. What is important for me is that some effort is made to 'codify' Nonya cuisine in an effort to preserve these recipes of yesteryear.

Western cuisine has reached great heights, thanks to the foundations laid down by the great culinary doyens such as Escoffier and Larousse. I owe a great deal to my grandmother, and those like her, for this rich culinary legacy. My hope is that the revised cookbooks do justice to her recipes.

Shermay

Shermay Lee
October 2004

soups

salads

Sotong Soup

Squid stuffed with minced pork in a clear soup

INGREDIENTS

500 g medium-sized squid
    (*sotong*)

2 cloves garlic (*bawang putih*)

1 spring onion (scallion)

1 sprig coriander (Chinese
    parsley) (*daun ketumbar*)

1 tbsp oil, optional

100 g glass noodles (*tunghoon*
    or *sohoon*)

800 ml water

$^1/_2$ tsp salt

a pinch of pepper

STUFFING

160 g minced pork

3 tsp light soy sauce

a pinch of salt

a dash of pepper

Tips:

- For a healthier version of this dish, use lean minced pork and substitute some pork with tofu.

- To make it easier to serve, break the glass noodles into shorter pieces before adding it to the stock or snip with a clean pair of scissors after it has cooked.

- Although not mentioned in my grandmother's original cookbook, you can clean and reattach the head of the squid to its body after stuffing it, if you prefer not to discard it. Alternatively, chop the soft parts of the squid tentacles and add it to the meat mixture.

PREPARATION

1 Remove and discard the head and tentacles, quill, ink sac and intestines from the squid. Using your fingers, pull off the reddish-brown skin from the squid tube then discard it. Rinse the tubes thoroughly in water. Drain and set aside.

2 Peel then mince the garlic.

3 Rinse then finely dice the spring onion and coriander.

METHOD

1 Heat a pot over a high flame until it smokes. Add the oil.

2 Lower the flame, then add the garlic. Stir-fry until light golden brown. Remove and drain well.

3 Return the garlic oil in the pot.

4 Prepare the stuffing. In a small bowl, add the fried garlic to the rest of the stuffing ingredients. Knead together until thoroughly mixed.

5 Fill the squid with the stuffing until it is about two-thirds full. (Do not overstuff the squid as it will shrink when cooked.) If there is any remaining stuffing, form small meatballs. Rub your hands with some of the garlic oil to form smooth meatballs, if preferred.

6 Add the water to the pot with the garlic oil.

7 Bring to the boil then add the stuffed squid and meatballs (if any). Simmer for 5–7 min.

8 Add the glass noodles. Simmer for another 3 min.

9 Season with salt and pepper to taste.

10 Turn off the flame then garnish with the diced spring onion and coriander.

Sook Muy Tong

Cream corn and minced chicken soup

This is a very easy soup to prepare since the ingredients are easy to obtain and inexpensive. I find that kids love it because it's tasty, easy to eat and bright yellow in colour.

INGREDIENTS

300 g minced chicken

$^{1}/_{2}$ tbsp Chinese cooking wine or sherry

$^{1}/_{2}$ tbsp salt

a dash of pepper

4 tbsp corn flour (cornstarch)

1 l chicken stock

2 eggs

425 g (1 can) cream corn

Tips:

- For a healthier version, prepare the minced chicken by using skinless chicken breasts then finely mincing it rather than buying ready-minced chicken.

- Using homemade chicken stock is also preferable. Alternatively, high quality, organic and MSG-free chicken stock is available in some stores.

- Although the recipe specifies using 1 can of cream corn, you can use less or more according to your preference.

PREPARATION

1 In a bowl with the minced chicken, add the wine or sherry, salt and pepper.

2 Dissolve the corn flour in 5 tbsp chicken stock, then add it to the minced chicken mixture. Combine.

3 Beat the eggs then set aside.

METHOD

1 In a large pot, bring the remaining chicken stock and cream corn to the boil.

2 Add the chicken mixture. Stir continually (to prevent it from clumping) while simmering for 3–5 min.

3 Turn off the flame then pour the beaten egg into the hot soup while stirring (which will result in a feathered effect). The residual heat in the soup will cook the egg.

4 Garnish with chopped spring onion or coriander (optional).

Pork Bone Soup

A soup of pork and potatoes seasoned with garlic, salted soy beans and ginger

This is a basic soup which is relatively simple to prepare. The ingredients are easy to obtain and the preparation time is relatively quick. The blue and white porcelain used to present this and other dishes (eg. Egg Foo Yong, Pork Chops and Hokkien Mee Soup) in this cookbook, was often used by my grandmother. It is a unique dining set with pieces suited for both Asian and Western dishes.

INGREDIENTS

300 g pork ribs

300 g potatoes

4 cloves garlic (*bawang putih*)

2 tbsp salted soy beans (*taucheo*)

3 tbsp oil

6 slices ginger (*halia*)

800 ml water

$^1/_2$ tsp salt

a dash of dark soy sauce

Tip:

For a really tasty soup, simmer for 1 hr or more over a low-medium heat, adding the potatoes only in the last 20 min of cooking time.

PREPARATION

1 Rinse then chop the pork ribs into medium-sized pieces.

2 Peel then cut the potatoes into cubes.

3 Peel then finely mince the garlic.

4 If whole salted soy beans are used, pound the beans.

METHOD

1 Heat a wok over a high flame until it smokes. Add the oil.

2 Lower the flame, then add the garlic and ginger. Stir-fry until light golden brown.

3 Add the salted soy beans, then sprinkle in some water to prevent it from burning.

4 Add the pork ribs and stir-fry. Sprinkle in more water.

5 Add the potatoes and stir-fry for 1 min.

6 Add the remaining water then bring to the boil. Simmer for 30 min, preferably more.

7 Add the salt and a dash of dark soy sauce to taste.

Rojak—Chinese Hawker's Style

Salad served with a peanut sauce

Possibly one of the most beloved of Singaporean dishes, Rojak has often been said to be representative of Singapore. Each ingredient is distinctive and different, much like our various races and languages, yet, these seemingly disparate ingredients combine to make a dish that is both unique and well-balanced.

Although it is a dish of Indonesian origin, Rojak has evolved into something that is entirely Singaporean with the use of Chinese doughsticks (*you char kway/you tiao*) and tofu puffs (*taupok*). The addition of finely shredded pink ginger bud is a Peranakan touch.

INGREDIENTS

1 small turnip (*bang kuang*)

¹/₂ pineapple

2 cucumbers

¹/₄ tsp bicarbonate of soda, optional

200 g bean sprouts (*tauge*)

160 g water convolvulus (*kangkung*)

1 pink ginger bud (*bunga siantan*)

4 pieces tofu puffs (*taupok*)

2 Chinese doughsticks (*you char kway/you tiao*)

DRESSING

2 fresh red chillies

1 tsp prawn (shrimp) paste (*belacan*)

1 kalamansi lime (*limau kesturi*) peel

1 tbsp kalamansi lime (*limau kesturi*) or lemon juice

4 tbsp raw palm sugar (*gula Melaka*)

2 tbsp black prawn (shrimp) paste (*haeko*)

¹/₂ tsp salt

8 tbsp peanuts (groundnuts), roasted and chopped

TAMARIND MARINADE

1 rounded tbsp tamarind (*asam*) pulp

8 tbsp water

PREPARATION

1 Peel then slice the turnip and pineapple into bite-sized pieces. Rinse then slice the cucumbers into similar sized pieces.

2 Bring some water to the boil then add the bicarbonate of soda before blanching the bean sprouts and then the water convolvulus separately. (The bicarbonate of soda will help the vegetables retain their colour.)

3 Finely slice the pink ginger bud using only the pink-coloured portion.

4 Grill or toast then slice the tofu and Chinese doughsticks.

5 Deseed, if preferred, then roughly chop the chillies.

6 Wrap the prawn paste in foil then toast in a dry pan or toaster for 1–2 min on each side. Remove the foil.

7 Finely shred the lime peel.

8 Prepare the tamarind marinade. (See page 193)

METHOD

1 Combine the dressing ingredients with the tamarind marinade. Mix well.

2 In a large bowl, toss the ingredients together with the dressing just before serving. Serve the Rojak on a large serving plate or on individual serving plates. Sprinkle the Rojak with the finely shredded pink ginger buds and chopped peanuts. Alternatively, place the ingredients in separate plates with the dressing on the side for everyone to mix their own.

Tip:
Toss the ingredients together just before serving as they will get soggy if allowed to sit for too long.

Rojak Java

Sticks of cucumber, turnip and pineapple served with a prawn paste dip

INGREDIENTS

2 cucumbers

600 g turnip (*bang kuang*)

1 pineapple

DIP

4 fresh red chillies

$1/2$ tbsp prawn (shrimp) paste (*belacan*)

$1/4$ tsp salt

6 tbsp palm sugar (*gula Melaka*)

1 tbsp black prawn (shrimp) paste (*haeko*)

TAMARIND MARINADE

1 rounded tbsp tamarind (*asam*) pulp

4 tbsp water

PREPARATION

1 Rinse then slice the cucumbers into sticks.

2 Peel then cut the turnip and pineapple into sticks.

3 Deseed, if preferred, then roughly chop the chillies.

4 Wrap the prawn paste in foil then toast in a dry pan or toaster oven for 1–2 min on each side. Remove the foil.

5 Prepare the tamarind marinade. (See page 193)

METHOD

1 Pound/grind all the ingredients for the dip together.

2 Combine the ingredients for the dip with the tamarind marinade. Mix well.

3 Arrange the cucumbers, turnip and pineapple sticks on a serving plate. Serve with the dip on the side.

Gado Gado

An Indonesian salad with a spicy peanut sauce

INGREDIENTS

200 g (2 heads) local lettuce
  (*sayur salad*)

2 cucumbers

1 kg cabbage

500 g long beans (*kacang
  panjang*)

500 g bean sprouts (*tauge*)

500 g potatoes

10 eggs

oil, for deep-frying

1.2 kg (6 pieces) firm tofu
  (*taukua*)

PEANUT SAUCE

1 l water

600 g peanuts (groundnuts),
  roasted and chopped

10 tbsp sugar

1^1/$_2$ tbsp salt

2 tbsp Chinese rice vinegar
  or white vinegar

REMPAH

25 dried red chillies
  or 6 fresh red chillies

10 shallots (*bawang merah*)

2 cloves garlic (*bawang putih*)

^{1}/$_2$ tbsp prawn (shrimp) paste
  (*belacan*)

GARNISH

fried sliced shallots (*bawang
  goreng*)

fried bitter nut crackers (*emping*)

Tip:

Instead of steaming the vegetables,
you may also parboil them. Simply
add ^{1}/$_4$ tsp of bicarbonate of soda to
the boiling water to help retain the
green colour. Prepare a large bowl of
cold water to plunge the blanched
vegetables into to prevent overcooking.

PREPARATION

1 If dried red chillies are used for the *rempah*, soak them in hot water.

2 Rinse then pat dry the local lettuce. Arrange on a large serving plate.

3 Rinse then slice the cucumbers diagonally into bite sized pieces. Arrange on the serving plate.

4 Slice the cabbage into 3 cm squares. Slice the long beans into 3 cm strips.

5 Remove and discard the caps and roots of the bean sprouts. Rinse and drain.

6 Prepare the *rempah*. Peel and roughly chop the shallots and garlic. Deseed, if preferred, then roughly chop the soaked/fresh chillies. Finely pound/grind all the *rempah* ingredients together. (See page 192)

METHOD

1 Using a steamer, boil the potatoes in the lower tier.

2 In the upper tier, steam the cabbage, long beans and bean sprouts separately. Arrange the vegetables on a serving plate.

3 Once the potatoes have cooked, remove then allow to cool. Peel then cut them into cubes. Arrange on a serving plate.

4 Hardboil the eggs in the lower tier of the steamer. Shell then slice the eggs into wedges. Arrange on a serving plate.

5 Heat a wok over a high flame until it smokes. Add some oil. Deep-fry the firm tofu until light golden brown. Remove and drain. Slice into cubes then arrange on a serving plate.

6 Discard the oil in the wok then heat some new oil (optional).

7 Add the *rempah* and stir-fry over a medium flame for 3–5 min.

8 Turn up the heat and add the water. Bring to the boil then add the chopped peanuts, salt, sugar and vinegar.

9 Simmer uncovered for about 10 min to allow the sauce to thicken. (The peanut oil will surface.) Allow the sauce to cool then serve on the side.

10 Garnish with fried shallots and bitter nut crackers.

Jaganan

An Indonesian salad with a spicy peanut sauce

Although Jaganan is very similar to Gado Gado, it requires fewer ingredients making it easier to prepare. The peanut sauce is also slightly different since it includes tamarind.

INGREDIENTS

¹/₄ tsp bicarbonate of soda

300 g bean sprouts (*tauge*)

300 g long beans (*kacang panjang*)

1 kg water convolvulus (*kangkung*)

6 eggs

oil, for deep-frying

1.2 kg (6 pieces) firm tofu (*taukua*)

PEANUT SAUCE

30 dried red chillies
or 7 fresh red chillies

4 kaffir lime leaves (*daun limau purut*)

4 tbsp prawn (shrimp) paste (*belacan*)

300 g peanuts (groundnuts), roasted and chopped

12 tbsp sugar

2 tsp salt

TAMARIND MARINADE

4 rounded tbsp tamarind (*asam*) pulp

650 ml water

> **Tip:**
> The cooking method of steaming used for Gado Gado can also be used here. Omit the use of bicarbonate of soda and steam the vegetables in the upper tier of the steamer and hardboil the eggs in the lower tier.

PREPARATION

1 If dried red chillies are used for the peanut sauce, soak them in hot water.

2 Remove and discard the caps and roots of the bean sprouts. Rinse and drain.

3 Slice the long beans into 3 cm strips.

4 Thoroughly rinse than pluck the tender portions of the water convolvulus. Discard the rest.

5 Roll the kaffir lime leaves together then finely slice.

6 Wrap the prawn paste in foil then toast in a dry pan or toaster oven for 1–2 min on each side. Remove the foil.

7 Prepare the tamarind marinade. (See page 193)

8 Prepare the peanut sauce. Deseed, if preferred, then roughly chop the soaked/fresh chillies and pound/grind with the prawn paste. Mix together with the remaining ingredients.

METHOD

1 Bring a pot of water to the boil. Add ¹/₄ tsp bicarbonate of soda to the boiling water before blanching the bean sprouts, long beans and water convolvulus in the water separately. (The bicarbonate of soda will help the vegetables retain their colour.) Plunge the vegetables in cold water to prevent overcooking, if preferred.

2 Drain well then arrange the vegetables on a large serving plate.

3 Hardboil the eggs in the same water. Allow to cool then shell and slice. Arrange on a serving plate.

4 Heat a wok over a high flame until it smokes. Add some oil. Deep-fry the firm tofu until light golden brown. Remove and drain. Slice into cubes and arrange on the serving plate.

5 Serve the peanut sauce on the side or toss the salad together then serve.

Tauhu Goreng

Fried tofu served with vegetables and a spicy peanut sauce

This dish is a combination of Chinese and Indonesian influences. Tofu is a widely used Chinese ingredient while the salad dressing is typically Indonesian.

INGREDIENTS

100 g bean sprouts (*tauge*)

1 cucumber

400 g (2 pieces) firm tofu (*taukua*)

oil, for deep-frying

PEANUT SAUCE

4 cloves garlic (*bawang putih*)

2 fresh red chillies

2 tbsp palm sugar (*gula Melaka*)

$1/4$ tsp salt

1 tbsp Chinese rice vinegar or white vinegar

2 tbsp dark soy sauce

8 tbsp water

160 g peanuts (groundnuts), roasted and chopped

Tip:
If palm sugar (*gula Melaka*) is not available, use brown sugar.

PREPARATION

1 Remove and discard the caps and roots of the bean sprouts. Rinse and drain.

2 Rinse then slice the cucumber.

3 Peel then roughly chop the garlic. Deseed, if preferred, then roughly chop the chillies. Pound/grind the garlic and chillies together.

4 Stir all the ingredients for the peanut sauce together until the sugar has dissolved.

METHOD

1 Blanch the bean sprouts in boiling water. Remove and drain.

2 Heat a wok over a high flame until it smokes. Add some oil. Deep-fry the firm tofu until light golden brown. Remove and drain.

3 Lay a few slices of cucumber on a plate, slice then place the tofu on top. Garnish with the bean sprouts.

4 Pour the peanut sauce over or serve it on the side.

snacks

Ngoh Hiang

Minced meat wrapped in tofu skin

Ngoh Hiang is considered a typical snack food in Singapore. It is commonly available at hawker stalls which also sell a wide range of other fried food including Chinese sausages, fried stuffed tofu and fish balls. These snacks are served with a bright and almost fluorescent pink coloured dipping sauce and chilli sauce.

INGREDIENTS
2 sheets dried tofu skin (*fupei*)
oil, for deep-frying

FILLING
8 water chestnuts
1 egg
160 g minced prawns (shrimps)
160 g minced pork
160 g minced pork belly
100 g crab meat
$1/2$ tsp salt
a dash of pepper

FLOUR PASTE
plain (all-purpose) flour
water

DIPPING SAUCES
chilli sauce, optional
sweet flour soy sauce
   (*timcheong*), optional

PREPARATION
1 Using a pair of scissors or a knife, cut the tofu skin into 15 cm squares, or slightly larger if preferred. Using a slightly damp cloth, wipe both sides to remove any dirt.
2 Rinse, peel then finely mince the water chestnuts. Beat the egg.
3 In a bowl, mix all the ingredients for the filling together.
4 Mix equal amounts of flour and water to form a small amount of paste.
5 Place a tofu skin on a clean dry surface with a corner pointing towards you. Spoon about 4 rounded tablespoonfuls of the filling in a row on the skin. Fold the corner of the skin facing you over the filling, then fold the left and right hand corners over it. Roll away from you to form a log about 12 cm long and 3 cm wide. Seal the end with a dab of the flour paste. Continue to make more rolls with the remaining ingredients.

METHOD
1 Heat some oil in a wok or pan over a medium-high flame.
2 Deep-fry the rolls until golden brown. Remove and drain well.
3 Slice each roll diagonally into 3 or 4 pieces. Place on a serving plate.
4 Serve with chilli sauce and/or sweet flour soy sauce on the side.

Tips:
- For a healthier version, replace the minced pork and minced pork belly with 320 g of minced lean pork. For a finer texture, finely mince the pork, pork belly and prawns together first before mixing.
- Some recipes for Ngoh Hiang recommend steaming the rolls for about 10 min before deep-frying. This ensures that the meat filling is cooked and prevents the skin from overbrowning. I find that you can skip the steaming if you deep-fry the rolls over a medium flame.

Lobah

Deep-fried rolls of shredded yam and meat

Some hawker stalls in Singapore still sell this as a snack. It is best eaten while still warm and dipped in chilli sauce. The outside should be crisp and golden brown, while the inside warm and moist—a perfect contrast to the spiciness and tanginess of the chilli sauce.

INGREDIENTS

600 g yam/taro (*keladi*)

300 g pork belly, optional

300 g prawns (shrimps)

1 small onion (*bawang*)

1 egg

12 tbsp (80 g) plain (all-purpose) flour

1 tsp sugar

1 tsp salt

oil, for deep-frying

DIPPING SAUCES

chilli sauce, optional

sweet flour soy sauce (*timcheong*), optional

> **Tip:**
> Serve Lobah with a chilli sauce called *cili cuka*. Pound some fresh red chillies then mix in a little vinegar, sugar and kalamansi lime juice.

PREPARATION

1 Peel then shred the yam/taro.

2 If pork belly is used, cut it into strips.

3 Peel, devein then mince the prawns.

4 Peel then finely dice the onion.

5 Beat the egg.

6 In a bowl, knead all the ingredients together (except for the oil, chilli sauce and sweet flour soy sauce).

7 Form into rolls about 12 cm long and 3 cm wide.

METHOD

1 Heat some oil in a wok or pan over a medium-high flame.

2 Deep-fry the rolls until golden brown. Remove and drain well.

3 Place on a serving plate. Serve with chilli sauce and/or sweet flour soy sauce on the side.

Rissoles

Breaded rolls of pancakes stuffed with meat and vegetables

This is an Indonesian dish of Dutch origin. It is particularly popular with kids because the fried breaded crust makes it crunchy on the outside, while the soft and tasty pancake and filling makes it soft and moist on the inside. It tastes good with ketchup, although the Singaporean preference is usually sweet chilli sauce.

INGREDIENTS

PANCAKE BATTER

100 g plain (all-purpose) flour

$^1/_4$ tsp salt

3 eggs

280 ml milk

1 tbsp oil

FILLING

1 onion (*bawang*)

100 g fresh or frozen green peas

1 tbsp corn flour (cornstarch)

2 tbsp water or milk

200 g minced pork

a pinch of nutmeg (*buah pala*) powder

$^1/_2$ tsp salt

a dash of pepper

2 tbsp oil

oil, for deep-frying

1 egg

breadcrumbs

DIPPING SAUCES

chilli sauce, optional

ketchup, optional

PREPARATION

Pancakes

1 Sift the flour and salt together then add the remaining ingredients for the batter. Use an electric whisk or whisk by hand until smooth.

2 Strain the batter, then set aside for at about 20 min to allow it to rest.

3 Using a non-stick or greased pan, make thin pancakes over a low flame. Set aside.

Filling

1 Peel then chop the onion. If frozen peas are used, defrost.

2 Mix the corn flour and water or milk together.

METHOD

1 Heat a wok over a medium flame. Add the oil.

2 Stir-fry or sweat the chopped onion then add the pork.

3 Season with nutmeg, salt and pepper.

4 Add the green peas and the corn flour mixture. Fry until the mixture is cooked and almost dry. Set aside to cool.

5 Lay a pancake on a clean dry surface. Place some filling on the pancake in a row. Fold the bottom end over the filling, then fold the left and right sides over. Roll the filling away from you towards the top. Continue to make more rolls with the remaining ingredients.

6 Prepare 2 deep dishes. Crack then beat the egg in one and fill the other with the breadcrumbs. Dip the rolls into the beaten egg then roll it in the breadcrumbs.

7 Heat some oil in a wok or pan over a medium-high flame. Deep-fry the rolls until light golden brown. Remove and drain well.

8 Place on a serving plate. Serve with chilli sauce or ketchup on the side.

Tip:

Roll the pancakes neatly and tightly to ensure that it does not unfold during frying. Coat it evenly with the beaten egg and cover it thoroughly with the breadcrumbs to ensure that the crust is even and sufficiently thick.

Fried Spring Rolls

Meat and shredded vegetables wrapped in crispy skin

Fried Spring Rolls are a tasty and popular snack and they can be filled with just about any ingredient. There are many interpretations of it across Asia—Chinese, Thai, Vietnamese and Filipino—to name a few. The Nonya version has a filling of bamboo shoots, a frequently used ingredient in our cuisine, and a combination of pork and prawns, which is also typical of Nonya recipes.

Healthier versions can be made by filling the rolls with more vegetables and cutting down or entirely omitting the meat. Luxurious versions can also be made by using more crab meat and good quality prawns.

INGREDIENTS

500 g spring roll sheets

oil, for deep-frying

FILLING

200 g small prawns (shrimps)

200 g pork

500 g cooked bamboo shoots (*rebung*)

5 dried Chinese mushrooms

$^1/_2$ thumb size knob ginger (*halia*)

4 spring onions (scallions)

3 tbsp oil

100 g crab meat

1 tbsp corn flour (cornstarch)

GRAVY

2 tbsp oyster sauce

1 tbsp light soy sauce

1 tbsp sugar

FLOUR PASTE

plain (all-purpose) flour

water

DIPPING SAUCES

chilli sauce, optional

ketchup, optional

PREPARATION

1 Shell, devein then dice the prawns.

2 Shred the pork and bamboo shoots.

3 Soak the Chinese mushrooms in hot water until softened. Squeeze dry. Discard the stem then finely slice the rest.

4 Peel and mince the ginger. Dice the spring onions.

5 In a small bowl, mix the gravy ingredients together.

6 Mix equal amounts of flour and water to form a small amount of paste.

METHOD

1 Heat a wok over a high flame until it smokes. Add the oil.

2 Stir-fry the ginger, pork and mushrooms for 1 min. Add the prawns.

3 Stir-fry then add the gravy. Add the bamboo shoots and crab meat.

4 Sprinkle the corn flour on top. Stir until the gravy has thickened.

5 Turn off the flame. Set aside to cool, then add the spring onions.

6 Lay a spring roll sheet on a clean dry surface with a corner facing toward you. Spoon some filling in a row on the skin. Fold the corner facing you over the filling, then fold the left and right hand corners over it. Roll away from you and seal with a dab of flour paste or water. Continue to make more rolls with the remaining ingredients.

7 Heat some oil in a wok or pan over a medium-high flame.

8 Deep-fry the rolls until light golden brown. Remove and drain well.

9 Place on a serving plate. Serve with chilli sauce or ketchup on the side.

Tip:

The filling can be prepared up to 2 days in advance. After preparing the filling, allow to cool, cover, then store in the refrigerator. Alternatively, make the spring rolls then freeze for up to 1 month. Deep-fry while still frozen when required.

Potato Balls

Deep-fried potato balls

INGREDIENTS

500 g potatoes
1 tbsp egg white, optional
$^1/_2$ tsp salt
oil, for deep-frying

DIPPING SAUCES
chilli sauce, optional
ketchup, optional

PREPARATION

1 In a large pot, boil the potatoes for about 30 min or until cooked.

2 Drain then allow to cool. Peel and discard the skin, then mash.

3 Mix in the egg white and salt.

4 Form the mixture into balls 3 cm in diameter.

METHOD

1 Heat some oil in a wok or pan over a medium-high flame.

2 Deep-fry the potato balls until light golden brown. Remove and drain well.

3 Place on a serving plate. Serve with chilli sauce or ketchup on the side.

Chicken/Pork Satay (Simplified)

Skewers of marinated and grilled chicken/pork

INGREDIENTS

500 g chicken or pork

20 satay sticks

REMPAH

4 shallots (*bawang merah*)

3 tbsp peanuts (groundnuts), roasted and chopped

2 tsp coriander (*ketumbar*) powder

$^1/_2$ tsp turmeric (*kunyit*) powder

$^1/_2$ tsp cinnamon powder

1 tbsp sugar

$^1/_2$ tsp salt

1 tbsp oil

Tips:

- For a healthier version, use skinless chicken breast then tenderise with the blunt edge of a cleaver. I prefer to use boneless thigh and drum meat since it is considered more tender.

- For pork satay, pork belly is traditionally used since it is a cheaper and juicier cut of meat, given its higher fat content. I prefer using pork fillet which is a leaner, healthier choice.

PREPARATION

1 Tenderise the meat by pounding slightly, if necessary. Cut into small cubes.

2 Peel then pound the shallots.

3 Mix all the ingredients for the *rempah* together. (See page 192)

4 Add the meat then knead together. Allow to marinate for 30 min or more.

5 Thread the meat using the satay sticks.

METHOD

1 Grill the satay over an open charcoal flame or on the top shelf of the oven at 240°C for 5–7 min on each side. Baste with oil on each side while grilling.

2 To serve, arrange the satay on a large serving plate with peeled and sliced onions or shallots, cucumbers and cubes of rice (*nasi tindeh* or *ketupat*) on the side. Serve the Chicken Satay with Peanut Satay Sauce (see page 42) and the Pork Satay with *Pineapple Satay Sauce.

*Pineapple Satay Sauce

A tangy pineapple dipping sauce for pork satay

Pork Satay goes perfectly with Pineapple Satay Sauce. The sauce only takes a little more effort to prepare, but makes all the difference to this dish. Pineapple Satay Sauce is traditionally served on its own or generously spooned on top of a bowl of Peanut Satay Sauce.

INGREDIENTS

$^1/_2$ pineapple

1 fresh red chilli, optional

$^1/_2$ tbsp sugar

1 tsp kalamansi lime (*limau kesturi*) or lemon juice

$^1/_4$ tsp salt

PREPARATION

1 Peel and grate the pineapple.

2 Pound the chilli, if used.

METHOD

1 Mix all the ingredients together and let it rest for about 15 min.

2 Serve in individual bowls or in a large serving bowl.

Beef/Mutton Satay (Simplified)

Skewers of marinated and grilled beef or mutton

INGREDIENTS

500 g beef or mutton

20 satay sticks

REMPAH

1 clove garlic (*bawang putih*)

2 slices ginger (*halia*)

4 shallots (*bawang merah*)

2 candlenuts (*buah keras*)

2 tsp coriander (*ketumbar*)
powder

1 tsp turmeric (*kunyit*) powder

1 tsp cumin (*jintan putih*)
powder

1 tsp salt

2 tbsp sugar

2 tbsp oil

3 tbsp peanuts (groundnuts),
roasted and chopped

PREPARATION

1 Tenderise the meat by pounding slightly, if necessary. Cut into small cubes.

2 Prepare the *rempah*. Peel then roughly chop the garlic, ginger and shallots. Pound/grind together with the remaining *rempah* ingredients. (See page 192)

3 Add the meat then knead together. Allow to marinate for 30 min or more.

4 Thread the meat using the satay sticks.

METHOD

1 Grill the satay over an open charcoal flame or on the top shelf of the oven at 240°C for 5–7 min on each side. Baste with oil on each side while grilling.

2 To serve, arrange the satay on a large serving plate with peeled and sliced onions or shallots, cucumbers and cubes of rice (*nasi tindeh* or *ketupat*) on the side. Serve with *Peanut Satay Sauce in individual bowls or in a large serving bowl.

*Peanut Satay Sauce (Simplified)

A moderately spicy peanut dipping sauce for beef, mutton and chicken satay

This recipe is enough for 80 sticks of satay or 2 kg of meat. Excess sauce can be stored in the freezer. Satay sauce now also comes ready-bottled or canned, but the quality varies with the brand. I find it handy to have a bottle or can in storage for when there is no time to prepare the sauce.

INGREDIENTS

6 cloves garlic (*bawang putih*)

2 stalks lemon grass (*serai*)

12 tbsp oil

2 tbsp pounded fresh chillies
or 1 tbsp chilli powder/flakes

500 g peanuts (groundnuts),
roasted and chopped

450 ml water

8 tbsp sugar

2 tbsp salt

TAMARIND MARINADE

1 rounded tbsp tamarind (*asam*)
pulp

130 ml water

PREPARATION

1 Peel then pound the garlic.

2 Peel then bruise the lemon grass (use white portion only).

3 Prepare the tamarind marinade. (See page 193)

METHOD

1 Heat a wok over a high flame until it smokes. Add the oil.

2 Lower the flame then stir-fry the garlic, pounded fresh chillies or chilli powder/flakes and the lemon grass.

3 Remove the lemon grass. Add the tamarind marinade, then simmer for 1 min.

4 Add the chopped peanuts and water.

5 Bring to the boil. Add the sugar and salt.

6 Simmer uncovered until the mixture has reduced and thickened (about 15 min).

Tip:

If roasted and ground peanuts are not available, substitute with peanut butter.

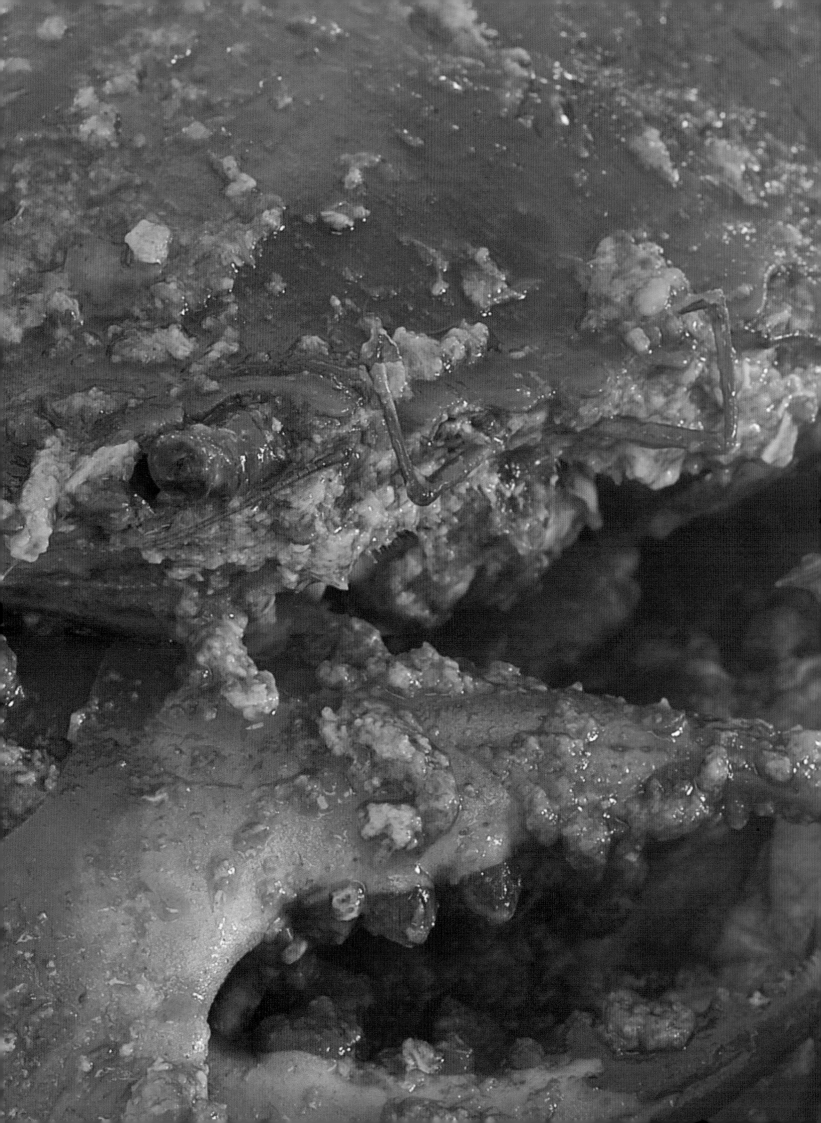

seafood

Chilli Crab

Crabs served in a mild chilli sauce

Chilli Crab is arguably one of the most iconic of Singapore dishes along with Chicken Rice, Laksa, Fish Head Curry and Char Kway Teow. For many, it also brings back memories of seaside restaurants and local beer. French loaves (baguette), Chinese buns (*mantou*) or rice is often served on the side and is used for soaking up the gravy.

INGREDIENTS

1.2 kg crabs

1 egg

8 tbsp oil

SAUCE

1 tbsp ketchup

2 tbsp sugar

1 tbsp salt

REMPAH

2 slices ginger (*halia*)

2 cloves garlic (*bawang putih*)

4 fresh red chillies

> **Tip:**
>
> Use high-quality live crabs, preferably Sri Lankan, to get the best out of this recipe. As an alternative, crabs can be substituted with lobsters or prawns, both of which go well with the spicy, tangy sweetness of the sauce.

PREPARATION

1 Prepare the crabs. Submerge the live crabs in ice cold water to immobilise them. Alternatively, place them in the refrigerator for about 30 min or pierce the main cavity with a chopstick. Thoroughly rinse the crab. Remove the pincers, the flap on the underside, then the back. Remove the spongy grey matter but retain the roe, if any. Chop the crabs into half then into smaller pieces, leaving the legs attached. Using a hammer or Chinese cleaver, crack the shell in several places (so that it will be easier to extract the meat later).

2 Beat the egg.

3 Mix all the ingredients for the sauce together.

4 Prepare the *rempah*. Peel the ginger and garlic, then roughly chop together with the chillies. Pound/grind the *rempah* ingredients together. (See page 192)

METHOD

1 Heat a wok over a high flame until it smokes. Add the oil.

2 Stir-fry the crab for 2 min then remove.

3 Over a medium flame, stir-fry the *rempah* for 2 min.

4 Add the crab to the wok then the sauce.

5 Turn off the flame then stir in the beaten egg. Serve immediately.

Sweet and Sour Crab

Crabs served in a tangy sweet and sour sauce

INGREDIENTS

1.2 kg crabs

6 tbsp oil

SAUCE

280 ml water

1^1/$_2$ tbsp dark soy sauce

2 tbsp Chinese rice vinegar
    or white vinegar

1^1/$_2$ tbsp sugar

^{1}/$_4$ tsp salt

REMPAH

20 shallots (*bawang merah*)

8 cloves garlic (*bawang putih*)

2 fresh red chillies

1 stalk lemon grass (*serai*)

GARNISHES

3 spring onions (scallions)

5 sprigs coriander (Chinese
    parsley) (*daun ketumbar*)

PREPARATION

1 Prepare the crabs. (See page 46)

2 Mix all the ingredients for the sauce together.

3 Peel then bruise the lemon grass (use white portion only).

4 Prepare the *rempah*. Peel the shallots and garlic, then roughly chop with the chillies. Pound/grind the *rempah* ingredients together, adding the bruised lemon grass last. (See page 192)

5 Rinse then shred the spring onions. Place the spring onions and coriander in cold water.

METHOD

1 Heat a wok over a high flame until it smokes. Add the oil.

2 Stir-fry the *rempah* until it turns light brown.

3 Add the crabs and sauce. Bring to the boil.

4 Simmer until the crabs are cooked (5–10 min).

5 Garnish with spring onions and coriander. Serve immediately.

Nonya Fish Curry

Fish in a curry sauce with vegetables

INGREDIENTS

600 g fish, such as Spanish mackerel (*ikan tenggiri*)

300 g eggplant (aubergine/ brinjal) or okra (ladies' fingers)

2 tomatoes

10 fresh green chillies

4 shallots (*bawang merah*)

4 cloves garlic (*bawang putih*)

$^1/_2$ thumb size knob ginger (*halia*)

10 tbsp oil

1 tsp sugar

1 tbsp salt

CURRY PASTE

8 tbsp Nonya fish curry powder

12 tbsp water

COCONUT MILK

125 g ($^1/_4$) grated coconut

450 ml water

(makes about 500 ml coconut milk)

TAMARIND MARINADE

$1^1/_2$ rounded tbsp tamarind (*asam*) pulp

250 ml water

PREPARATION

1 Rinse then cut the fish into pieces.

2 If eggplant is used, cut it into cubes or thick slices then soak in water (to prevent discolouring). If okra is used, trim the stem then use them whole.

3 Cut the tomato into quarters.

4 Slit the fresh green chillies lengthwise then deseed, if preferred.

5 Peel then slice the shallots, garlic and ginger.

6 Mix the curry powder and water into a paste.

7 Prepare the coconut milk. (See page 193)

8 Prepare the tamarind marinade. (See page 193)

METHOD

1 Heat a wok over a high flame until it smokes. Add the oil.

2 Reduce to a lower flame then stir-fry the garlic.

3 When the garlic is half-cooked, add the shallots.

4 When the shallots are half-cooked, add the ginger.

5 Stir-fry until it is light golden brown, then add 3 tbsp coconut milk and the curry paste.

6 Simmer for 3 min, stirring constantly then add another 3 tbsp coconut milk.

7 Add the remaining coconut milk, tamarind marinade, sugar and salt.

8 Bring to the boil. Add the fish and vegetables.

9 Simmer for about 10 min over a low-medium flame.

Chow Har

Large prawns fried in a tomato sauce

This is a quick and easy-to-cook and Cantonese dish. As with other Cantonese dishes, the freshness of the ingredients is crucial since the cooking style is simple.

INGREDIENTS

1 kg large prawns (shrimps)

1 tsp salt

12 spring onions (scallions)

8 tbsp oil

SAUCE

1 tbsp oyster sauce

100 g ginger (*halia*)

1 tbsp Chinese cooking wine or sherry

6 tbsp ketchup

$1/2$ tbsp corn flour (cornstarch)

2 tbsp water

$1^1/_2$ tbsp sugar

1 tsp salt

GARNISHES

1 cucumber, optional

1 tomato, optional

PREPARATION

1 Using a pair of scissors, trim the feelers and sharp tips of the prawns. Using a sharp knife, make an incision on the back of the prawns cutting through the shell then remove the vein. Season with salt.

2 Cut the spring onions into short strips then shred.

3 Peel then pound/grind the ginger. Squeeze over a sieve or using a muslin bag to extract 1 tbsp juice.

4 Slice the cucumber and tomato. Arrange alternately on the edge of a serving plate.

METHOD

1 In a pot, mix the ingredients for the sauce. Bring to the boil, then simmer until the sauce has thickened.

2 Heat a wok over a high flame until it smokes. Add the oil.

3 When the oil starts to smoke, add the prawns. Stir-fry for about 3 min.

4 Pour the sauce over the prawns. Quickly toss together. Add the shredded spring onions then remove from heat.

5 Place on the prepared serving plate.

Asam Sotong Goreng

Squid marinated in a tangy tamarind marinade stir-fried in its own ink

This is an unusual dish to some because the ink of the squid is used to make the gravy. However, there are many who like it precisely because of the squid ink, not to mention that this is a very simple dish to prepare.

INGREDIENTS

300 g small squids (*sotong*)

5 tbsp oil

1 tbsp salt

TAMARIND MARINADE

1 rounded tbsp tamarind (*asam*) pulp

570 ml water

Tips:
- If small squids are not available, medium or large squids can be used.
- Squids cook quickly, so be careful not to overcook, as they tend to toughen if overdone.

PREPARATION

1 Prepare squids by first pulling away the tentacles. The eye, ink sac and intestines will follow. Remove the quill and discard. Reserve the tentacles by cutting just above the eye and discarding the rest. Cut the tentacles into smaller pieces. Reserve the ink sac but discard the head. Be careful not to burst the ink sac. Rinse the squids in cold water. Do this twice if necessary.

2 Prepare the tamarind marinade. (See page 193)

3 Add the squids to the marinade then set aside for 30 min or more.

Method

1 Drain the squids using a sieve. Discard the marinade.

2 Heat a wok over a high flame until it starts to smoke. Add the oil.

3 Once the oil is very hot, add the squid.

4 Fry the squids for 1–2 min to release the ink. Remove the squids and set aside.

5 Allow the remaining liquid to reduce as the black squid ink surfaces (3–5 min). This allows the sauce to thicken without overcooking the squid.

6 Return the squids to the wok and fry for another 1–2 min.

7 Season with salt to taste.

Fish with Mixed Vegetables

Chinese stir-fried dishes are very easy to prepare and relatively healthy, since little oil is used. It is important not to overcook the vegetables but to have them just done, or as the Italians say, *al dente*.

In Chinese restaurants, the intense heat from the wok gives the dishes a very distinct flavour which the Cantonese call *wok hei*.

INGREDIENTS

500 g fish, preferably red
   snapper (*ikan merah*)

1 carrot

200 g broccoli/long or French
   beans/green pepper/
   cauliflower

6 water chestnuts

150 g (1 small can) button
   mushrooms

800 ml oil

6 slices ginger (*halia*)

6 slices cooked bamboo shoots
   (*rebung*) or 100 g cauliflower

MARINADE

1 egg white

1 tsp bicarbonate of soda

$1/2$ tsp sugar

$1/2$ tsp salt

a dash of pepper

GRAVY

2 tsp Chinese cooking wine
   or sherry

4 tsp light soy sauce

1 tsp sesame oil

8 tbsp water

1 tbsp corn flour (cornstarch)

1 tsp sugar

$1/2$ tsp salt

Tip:

Keep the wok over a medium to high heat since this will quickly cook the vegetables and retain their texture and nutrients, as with blanching.

PREPARATION

1 Cut the fish into small thick slices.

2 Mix the ingredients for the marinade. Add the fish. Mix well together.

3 Peel, slice and separately blanch the carrot and broccoli/long or French beans/ green pepper/cauliflower.

4 Rinse, peel then slice the water chestnuts.

5 Drain and rinse the canned button mushrooms.

6 Mix the ingredients for the gravy together.

METHOD

1 Heat a wok over a high flame until it smokes. Add half the oil, then heat it until it smokes. Turn off the flame then add the remaining oil. (This procedure for preparing the oil provides the perfect temperature for frying fish.)

2 Add the fish. The fish is cooked once it has surfaced to the top. Remove and drain the fish. Pour off the oil, reserving 2 tbsp in the wok.

3 Reheat the wok. Stir-fry the ginger then all the vegetables, except the mushrooms.

4 Add the mushrooms, fried fish then gravy.

5 Bring to the boil, then simmer until the sauce thickens (about 10 min).

6 Remove and place on a serving plate.

Foo Yong Hai

An omelette with crab meat, ham and bamboo shoots

This is probably one of the dishes that my grandmother learnt from Cantonese Chef Tham Yui Kai. Foo Yong Hai is a common dish prepared at Chinese home-style restaurants (*zicha*) and in Chinese homes in Singapore. There are several ways of preparing this dish. This one is particularly elaborate. Nevertheless, it is well worth the effort since it results in a delicious crispy edge with a whole fried egg in the centre.

INGREDIENTS

350 g cooked bamboo shoots (*rebung*)

100 g ham

4 spring onions (scallions)

500 g crab meat, flaked

1 tsp pepper

6 eggs

10 tbsp oil

EGG MIXTURE

4 eggs

$^1/_2$ tbsp sugar

1 tbsp salt

1 tbsp sesame oil

4 tbsp oil

Tips:

- For a healthier version, reduce or omit the egg yolks and substitute with more egg whites.
- For an easier version, make a standard omelette or scramble the egg mixture.

PREPARATION

1 Shred the bamboo shoots. Squeeze out any excess water.

2 Shred the ham and spring onions.

3 On a large plate, spread out the bamboo shoots, crab meat, ham and spring onions. Sprinkle the pepper over.

4 Combine all the ingredients for the egg mixture, beat together then pour it over the assembled ingredients. Using a spoon, stir the mixture to form 6 small nests. Break an egg into each nest.

METHOD

1 Heat a wok over a high flame until it smokes. Add the oil.

2 When the oil is very hot, slide a nest into the oil.

3 Stir-fry in one direction until the eggs are set.

4 Turn the omelette over then fry the other side.

5 Serve garnished with chopped spring onions or a sprig of coriander (optional).

chicken
and duck

Chicken Wrapped in Paper

Marinated chicken deep-fried in a paper parcel

Also known as *ji bao gai*, literally, 'paper-wrapped chicken' in Cantonese, this dish is believed to have been first created in a Chinese restaurant in Singapore. It is one of my favourite recipes since it is rather fail-proof, tasty and quick to prepare. Perfect for busy mothers who have to whip up dinner after work.

INGREDIENTS

800 g chicken meat

oil, for deep-frying

MARINADE

100 g ginger (*halia*)

100 g onion (*bawang*)

1 tbsp light soy sauce

1 tbsp corn flour (cornstarch)

2 tbsp water

1 tsp sesame oil

4 tbsp oil

1 tsp sugar

1 tsp salt

12 pieces of greaseproof or
    baking paper, cut into
    15 cm squares

Tip:

The chicken can be marinated and wrapped then refrigerated the day before or frozen until required.

PREPARATION

1 Cut the chicken into small pieces.

2 Prepare the marinade. Peel then pound/grind the ginger and onion separately. Squeeze over a sieve or using a muslin bag to extract 1 tbsp juice from each. In a large bowl, mix all the marinade ingredients together. Add the chicken to the marinade. Knead then set aside to marinate for at least 30 min.

3 Wrap each piece of chicken in paper to form neat parcels. Place the paper such that one corner points towards you. Spoon some marinated chicken onto the middle then fold the corner facing you over the chicken. Fold the left and right corners in then fold the remaining corner over and tuck it into the fold.

METHOD

1 Heat a wok over a high flame until it smokes. Add the oil.

2 Deep-fry the chicken parcels in batches of 2 or 3 for about 5 min per batch. Flip the parcel over once to ensure even cooking of the chicken. Remove and drain.

3 Serve immediately (with the paper wrapping).

Crispy Fried Chicken

Chicken, marinated in soy sauce and spices, with a crispy crust

INGREDIENTS

1 medium-sized chicken (about
    1 kg) or 800 g chicken meat

12 tbsp corn flour (cornstarch)

oil, for deep-frying

MARINADE

1 tbsp light soy sauce

1 tbsp Chinese cooking wine
    or sherry

1 tsp five spice powder

1 tbsp corn flour (cornstarch)

6 tbsp water

1 tbsp sugar

1 tbsp salt

PREPARATION

1 Cut the chicken into pieces.

2 In a large bowl, mix the marinade ingredients together. Add the chicken to the
   marinade. Knead then set aside to marinate for 30 min or more.

3 Toss the chicken in corn flour just before frying.

METHOD

1 Heat a wok over a high flame until it smokes. Add the oil.

2 Once the oil starts to smoke, turn off or lower the flame. Add the chicken and
   deep-fry.

3 Turn the flame on again and continue to deep-fry until the chicken is golden
   brown. Remove and drain well.

Yok Lan Gai

Chicken served with ham, broccoli and gravy

The Chinese traditionally prepare a similar dish without the vegetables and gravy for ceremonial presentations. The parents of a one-month old child may also present this dish to their relatives and friends as a token of appreciation for the gifts received during the birth of the child. The whole chicken, including the head and feet would be presented, since it represents wholesomeness and fullness. Ten hardboiled eggs dyed red would also be included as they are believed to symbolise abundance and fertility.

This is an adapted version of the traditional dish and is suitable for home meals with family and friends. It is very likely that my grandmother learnt to prepare this dish from Chef Tham Yui Kai as it is a classic Cantonese dish one would expect to have at a grand 12-course banquet.

INGREDIENTS

1 medium-sized chicken (about 1 kg)

100 g ham

600 g broccoli or asparagus (12 florets of broccoli or 12 spears of asparagus)

GRAVY

50 g ginger (*halia*)

300 ml chicken stock

1 tbsp light soy sauce

$1/2$ tbsp Chinese cooking wine or sherry

1 tbsp corn flour (cornstarch)

1 tbsp oil

$1/2$ tsp salt

PREPARATION

1 Clean and drain the chicken. Slit the leg tendons so that the legs can be bent.

2 Slice the ham into 3 cm squares.

3 Peel then pound/grind the ginger. Squeeze over a sieve or using muslin bag to extract $1/2$ tbsp juice. In a pot, mix the ingredients for the gravy together.

METHOD

1 Fill a large pot with enough water to immerse the chicken. Bring the water to the boil.

2 Hold the chicken by the legs and place it into the boiling water for about 3 min. Remove and drain. Cool for about 3 min while the water comes to the boil again. Repeat this process again.

3 Place the chicken breast-side down. Cover and boil for about 2 min. Turn off the flame.

4 Allow the chicken to sit in the water for about 30 min. Remove then dip the chicken into a basin of cold water. Hang the chicken to dry.

5 Bring the chicken stock to the boil. Blanch the broccoli or asparagus.

6 Cut the chicken into pieces.

7 On a large serving plate, arrange the chicken, broccoli or asparagus and ham.

8 Bring the gravy to the boil then simmer until it has thickened. Pour the gravy over the dish. Serve immediately.

Chicken Filling in a Yam Basket

Chicken stir-fried with mixed vegetables

It is highly probable that my grandmother learnt to make this dish from Chef Tham Yui Kai since this is the type of dish that would be served in a Cantonese restaurant or at a Cantonese-style Chinese banquet.

INGREDIENTS

600 g boneless chicken
3 dried Chinese mushrooms
2 stalks celery
4 slices cooked bamboo shoots (*rebung*)
1 green capsicum (bell pepper)
4 fresh red chillies or 1 red capsicum (bell pepper)
iceberg lettuce
6 tbsp oil

MARINADE

6 tbsp water
1 tbsp egg white
1 tbsp corn flour (cornstarch)
1 tsp bicarbonate of soda
1 1/2 tsp sugar
1 tsp salt

GRAVY

1 tsp light soy sauce
1 tsp oyster sauce
1/2 tsp sesame oil
1 tbsp Chinese cooking wine or sherry
1/2 tbsp corn flour (cornstarch)
5 tbsp water
1 tsp sugar
1/2 tsp salt
a dash of pepper

PREPARATION

1 Cut the chicken into small pieces.
2 Mix the ingredients for the marinade. Add the chicken. Knead together.
3 Soak the Chinese mushrooms in hot water until softened. Squeeze dry. Discard the stems then finely slice the rest.
4 Slice the celery, bamboo shoots and capsicum. If fresh red chillies are used, slice into square pieces (deseed, if preferred).
5 Finely shred then arrange the lettuce on a serving plate, then place the *Yam Basket on top.
6 Mix all the gravy ingredients together in a bowl.

METHOD

1 Heat a wok over a high flame until it smokes. Add the oil.
2 When the oil is hot, turn off the flame. Add the chicken and stir-fry for half a min.
3 Pour the chicken and oil in a colander. Discard the oil. Set aside the chicken.
4 Reheat the wok over a high flame, then add 3 tbsp oil.
5 Stir-fry the celery, mushrooms and bamboo shoots. Add the capsicum and chillies.
6 Add the chicken. Stir-fry for 1 min then add the gravy. Bring to the boil.
7 Turn off the flame then scoop the mixture into the Yam Basket. Serve immediately.

---

*Yam Basket

A basket made of shredded yam

INGREDIENTS

750 g yam/taro (*keladi*) or potatoes
4 tbsp corn flour (cornstarch)
oil, for deep-frying

2 round perforated ladles

PREPARATION

1 Peel then slice the yam/taro or potatoes into thin strips.
2 Line one ladle with the strips. Dust with corn flour. Press the other ladle on top then trim off any excess strips along the edge to neaten, if necessary.

METHOD

1 Heat a wok over a high flame until it smokes. Add the oil.
2 Shake the ladles to remove any excess corn flour.
3 Lower to a medium flame then immerse the ladles in the oil.
4 Deep-fry for about 3 min or until the basket is light golden brown.
5 Remove, carefully unmould then allow to drain on kitchen paper.
6 Allow to cool then store in an airtight container for use as required.

Chicken with Mixed Vegetables

Stir-fried chicken with mixed vegetables

INGREDIENTS

300 g chicken meat

500 g green capsicums
(bell peppers)

100 g cooked bamboo shoots
(*rebung*)

100 g carrots

150 g (1 can) button mushrooms

4 fresh red chillies

3 tbsp oil

8 tbsp water

MARINADE

2 tsp corn flour (cornstarch)

2 tsp light soy sauce

2 tsp water

SAUCE

100 g ginger (*halia*) or 1 tsp
ginger powder

1 thumb size knob ginger (*halia*)

2 tbsp light soy sauce

$^1/_2$ tbsp sesame oil

1 tbsp corn flour (cornstarch)

8 tbsp water

$^1/_2$ tbsp sugar

$^1/_2$ tbsp salt

Tip:

If preferred, you may omit any one of
these vegetables as it will not affect
the final dish significantly. Typically,
4–6 ingredients are used to give the
dish variety. Vegetables such as
broccoli, cauliflower and Chinese
mushrooms can also be added. For
variety, substitute chicken with prawns
(shrimps) or pork.

PREPARATION

1 Cut the chicken into small pieces.

2 Mix the ingredients for the marinade together. Add the chicken. Knead together.

3 Slice the capsicums, bamboo shoots and carrots into small thin pieces.

4 Slice the button mushrooms into half.

5 Deseed, if preferred, then slice the chillies.

6 If fresh ginger is used, peel then pound/grind the 100 g ginger and squeeze over a
sieve or using muslin bag to extract 1 tbsp juice.

7 Peel then finely shred the 1 thumb size of fresh ginger, if used.

8 Mix the ingredients for the sauce together. Set aside.

METHOD

1 Heat a wok over a high flame until it smokes. Add the oil.

2 Stir-fry the carrots, bamboo shoots, capsicums then chillies.

3 Add the mushrooms then the chicken.

4 Add the water. Lower to a medium flame, cover and simmer for 2 min.

5 Remove the lid, stir-fry for 2 min. Add the sauce.

6 Bring to the boil, then simmer until the sauce thickens (about 10 min).

7 Remove and place on a serving plate.

Chicken and Cashew Nuts

Stir-fried chicken and cashew nuts

This is probably another dish that my grandmother learnt from Chef Tham Yui Kai who used to preside at the popular Cathay Restaurant on the fourth floor of Cathay Building in Singapore. Sadly, the restaurant has now closed its doors. During its heyday, it was one of the first to introduce Hong Kong Cantonese cuisine to Singapore, which was, and still is, considered very refined and sophisticated.

Chicken and Cashew Nuts is a typical Cantonese restaurant dish which can be easily replicated in a domestic kitchen—unlike some of the other dishes which are technically more difficult to do.

INGREDIENTS

500 g chicken meat

200 g cashew nuts

1 tsp bicarbonate of soda

water

$^1/_2$ tsp sugar

$^1/_2$ tsp salt

850 ml oil

MARINADE

1 tsp bicarbonate of soda

1 tsp sugar

4 tbsp water

$1^1/_2$ tbsp egg white

1 tbsp corn flour (cornstarch)

2 tbsp oil

SAUCE

1 tsp oyster sauce

1 tsp dark soy sauce

1 tsp light soy sauce

$^1/_2$ tsp sesame oil

$^1/_2$ tbsp corn flour (cornstarch)

8 tbsp water

2 tsp sugar

$^1/_2$ tsp salt

a dash of pepper

PREPARATION

1 Cut the chicken into small pieces.

2 Mix the ingredients for the marinade together, except for the corn flour and oil. Add the chicken. Knead together then add the corn flour and oil. Set aside.

3 Soak the cashew nuts in bicarbonate of soda mixed with 2 tbsp water. Drain then rinse well.

4 Bring to the boil about 300 ml water, sugar and salt.

5 Blanch the cashew nuts. Remove and drain well. Set aside.

6 Combine all the ingredients for the sauce.

METHOD

1 Heat a wok over a high flame until it smokes. Add the oil.

2 Once the oil is hot, turn off the flame. Stir-fry the cashew nuts until light golden brown. Remove and drain well. Set aside.

3 Reheat the oil over a high flame then add the chicken. Remove and drain. Discard the oil.

4 Reheat the wok over a high flame, stir-fry the chicken and add the sauce.

5 Bring to the boil then turn off the flame. Stir in the cashew nuts. Serve immediately.

Tip:
For variety, add celery, carrots or canned button mushrooms. You can also use macadamia nuts instead of cashew nuts.

Ayam Tempra

Chicken glazed in a soy sauce and lime juice sauce

This is a good recipe for new cooks or those who are living overseas and longing for Asian food since the ingredients are easy to obtain and the cooking method is simple.

INGREDIENTS

1 medium-sized chicken (about 1 kg) or 1 kg chicken pieces

2 onions (*bawang*)

4 fresh red chillies

6 tbsp oil

4 tbsp sugar

4 tbsp dark soy sauce

4 tbsp kalamansi lime (*limau kesturi*) or lemon juice

1/2 tsp salt

50 ml water

Tips:

- This recipe can also be used for pork and fish. Substitute the chicken with pork (600 g) to make Babi Tempra and fish (300 g) to make Ikan Tempra.

- For Ikan Tempra, fry the fish in some oil then drain and discard the oil. In the same wok, add another 6 tbsp oil then fry the other ingredients. Once the sauce is ready, add the fried fish. Do not add water. Coat the fish well with the sauce then serve.

PREPARATION

1 If a whole chicken is used, rinse and cut the chicken into small pieces.

2 Peel then thinly slice the onions.

3 Peel then slice the chillies (deseed, if preferred).

METHOD

1 Heat a wok over a high flame until it smokes. Add the oil.

2 Stir-fry the onions until slightly softened.

3 Add the chillies then the chicken.

4 When the chicken is half-cooked, add the sugar.

5 Lower to a medium flame, then add the dark soy sauce, lime or lemon juice and salt.

6 When the chicken is cooked, add the water then simmer for a few min.

7 Remove and place on a serving bowl or plate.

Grilled Chicken

Marinated chicken wrapped with bacon and grilled

This is another dish with Western and Asian influences from Singapore's British colonial past. It was probably created in the kitchen of one of the British social clubs or colonial bungalows, or a Hainanese restaurant serving standard Western fare. The use of bacon is Western while the marinade consisting of shallots, Chinese cooking wine and light soy sauce is Asian. The cooking method also seems to borrow elements from both cultures.

INGREDIENTS

1 medium-sized chicken (about 1 kg)
oil, for deep-frying
2 slices bacon
10 tbsp water

MARINADE

5 shallots (*bawang merah*)
1 clove garlic (*bawang putih*)
1 tsp Chinese cooking wine or sherry
1 tsp light soy sauce
2 tbsp water
1 tsp salt

PREPARATION

1 Rinse then cut the chicken into half lengthwise.
2 Peel then pound the shallots and garlic. Squeeze together over a sieve or using a muslin bag to extract about 1 tsp juice.
3 Mix the ingredients for the marinade together then add the chicken. Marinate for 30 min or more.

METHOD

1 Heat a wok over a high flame until it smokes. Add the oil.
2 Once the oil is very hot, deep-fry the chicken for 3 min on each side or until the chicken is light golden brown on the surface.
3 Remove and drain the chicken. Drain the oil from the wok.
4 Place the chicken in the wok, skin-side facing up.
5 Place the bacon on the chicken then add the water.
6 Cover and simmer for 20–30 min.
7 Remove then grill the chicken in the oven at 200°C for 10 min or until the bacon is crisp.

Boneless Stuffed Chicken

Boneless whole chicken roasted with a ham, mushroom and minced pork stuffing

Boneless Stuffed Chicken is an impressive and very tasty dish that is suitable for serving at parties or family meals. It is rather elaborate since it requires that a whole chicken be deboned with its skin intact. The chicken can then be sliced at the table, displaying a cross section of the chicken and the stuffing.

This is yet another dish that Singapore has inherited from her colonial past. The use of butter, bread, ham, Worcestershire sauce and milk are clearly Western, while the use of light soy sauce is undoubtedly Asian.

When I first came across this recipe in my grandmother's cookbook, I was puzzled by the instructions and had difficulty visualising the final dish as I had never had this dish before. Fortunately, a few of my older cousins remembered it and so I could rely on them to help me recreate this dish. I believe few Nonyas during my grandmother's time, and more so now, knew how to debone an entire chicken. I learnt how to debone poultry while I was attending professional French culinary classes, and even then, 'tunnel boning' was considered a classic art or 'old school'. Fortunately, I know a butcher who can tunnel bone a chicken (see Useful Contacts, page 198).

INGREDIENTS

1 large chicken (1.2–1.4 kg with bones)

4 eggs

2 tbsp light soy sauce

2 tbsp butter

STUFFING

2 slices bread

100 g ham

150 g (1 can) button mushrooms

1 onion (*bawang*)

500 g minced pork

1 egg

2 tsp Chinese cooking wine or sherry

1 tsp Worcestershire sauce

1 tbsp light soy sauce

8 tbsp milk

1 tsp salt

$^1/_2$ tsp pepper

a pinch of nutmeg (*buah pala*), grated or powdered

cooking string

trussing needle

PREPARATION

1 Tunnel bone/debone the entire chicken while keeping it whole, by scrapping and pulling the meat away from the bones through the open cavity. Remove the rib cage first followed by each of its limbs. Rinse then pat dry the chicken.

2 Hardboil then shell the eggs.

3 Slice off the crust, if preferred, then soak the bread in water. Squeeze out the excess water then mash.

4 Dice the ham and mushrooms.

5 Peel, dice then fry the onion until golden brown.

6 Mix all the ingredients for the stuffing together.

7 Stuff the mixture and the boiled eggs into the cavity of the chicken. Seal the opening of the cavity with toothpicks or by sewing it together with cooking string. (Any extra stuffing can be fried then served with the chicken on the side.)

8 Rub the skin of the chicken with the light soy sauce and butter.

METHOD

1 Preheat oven to 180°C. Roast the chicken for about 40 min to 1 hr (depending on the size of the chicken). Turn the chicken over halfway during the cooking process.

2 Remove then allow the chicken to rest for 10–15 min before serving.

Chicken Stew

Chicken stewed with potatoes, carrots and tomatoes

Chicken Stew is a dish that reflects Singapore's British colonial past. This recipe is an Asian interpretation of a Western chicken stew or casserole. Corn flour is used to thicken the stew, which is typical of Chinese cooking, and soy sauce, an unmistakably Asian seasoning, is also added. Chicken stew is commonly served with white rice.

INGREDIENTS

1 medium-sized chicken (about 1 kg) or 1 kg chicken pieces

300 g potatoes

300 g carrots

2 tomatoes

1 onion (*bawang*)

4 shallots (*bawang merah*)

3 tbsp oil

3 cm stick cassia bark (*kayu manis*) or a pinch of cinnamon powder

2 tsp sugar

1^1/$_2$ tsp salt

850 ml water

MARINADE

1 tbsp dark soy sauce

a dash of pepper

CORN FLOUR MIXTURE

2 tbsp corn flour (cornstarch)

6 tbsp water

Tip:
My personal preference is to use chicken drumsticks and thighs for this dish, but skinless chicken breasts can also be used for a healthier option. Add 2 bay leaves, if preferred.

PREPARATION

1 If a whole chicken is used, rinse then cut the chicken into pieces.

2 Rub the dark soy sauce and pepper over the chicken. Leave to marinate.

3 Peel then cut the potatoes and carrots into cubes.

4 Quarter the tomatoes. Peel and quarter the onion.

5 Peel and finely pound the shallots.

6 Mix the corn flour and water together.

METHOD

1 Heat a wok over a high flame until it smokes. Add the oil.

2 Reduce the flame. Stir-fry the shallots then add the chicken.

3 Add the potatoes, carrots, tomatoes and onion.

4 Add the remaining ingredients, except the corn flour mixture.

5 Bring to the boil then simmer until the chicken is cooked (30–40min).

6 Thicken the stew with the corn flour mixture by stirring it in about 10 min before the chicken is cooked.

Nonya Chicken Curry

A basic Nonya chicken curry

Chicken curry is a dish common in many Asian cultures. Indian and Thai versions, for instance, are well-known and well-loved. It is interesting how each of these cultures uses similar ingredients and cooking methods but with differing results. In general, Nonya curry tends to be creamier and richer given the large quantities of coconut milk used (much like Malay curries), but less spicy than the Indian curries and less 'chilli hot' than the typical Thai curry.

INGREDIENTS

1 medium-sized chicken (about 1 kg) or 1 kg chicken pieces

1 onion (*bawang*)

12 tbsp oil

2 tsp salt

MARINADE

8 tbsp Nonya chicken curry powder

8 tbsp water

4 shallots (*bawang merah*)

4 cloves garlic (*bawang putih*)

4 slices ginger (*halia*)

COCONUT MILK

250 g ($^1/_2$) grated coconut

450 ml water

(makes about 550 ml coconut milk)

PREPARATION

1 If a whole chicken is used, rinse then cut the chicken into pieces.

2 Peel then slice the onion.

3 Prepare the marinade. Mix the curry powder and water into a paste. Peel then pound the shallots, garlic and ginger together. Add to the curry paste then rub the marinade on the meat. Leave in the refrigerator for 1 hr or more.

4 Prepare the coconut milk. (See page 193)

METHOD

1 Heat a wok over a high flame until it smokes. Add the oil.

2 Stir-fry the onion until light golden brown.

3 Add 5 tbsp coconut milk and the chicken with the marinade.

4 Stir-fry for 2 min, then add 5 tbsp coconut milk.

5 Simmer for 3 min, then add the remaining coconut milk.

6 Bring to the boil then simmer uncovered until the chicken is cooked (20–30 min).

7 Season with salt to taste. Serve with *Roti Jala or white rice.

*Roti Jala

A thin lacy pancake

A special piece of kitchen equipment, called the *acuan roti jala* in Malay is used to dispense the batter (see Basic Kitchen Equipment, page 196). If you are unable to obtain one, use a disposable plastic cup and poke holes at the base. Alternatively, dip your fingers into the batter, then drizzle the batter onto the pan. It may be messy, but it works.

INGREDIENTS

BATTER

200 g plain (all-purpose) flour

3 eggs

$^1/_2$ tsp fine salt

400 ml milk

2 tbsp oil

oil, for greasing

PREPARATION

1 Sift the flour to remove any lumps. Repeat, if necessary.

2 Mix all the batter ingredients together.

3 Beat the batter until it is smooth. Strain to remove any lumps. Set the mixture aside to rest for a least 20 min. (Place it in the refrigerator if it is left to rest for longer.)

METHOD

1 Lightly grease a crepe pan or flat pan with oil. Heat over a low-medium flame.

2 Scoop some batter up using the Roti Jala dispenser.

3 Using a circular motion, drizzle the batter onto the pan to form a thin lacy pancake. Hold a small plate or bowl underneath the dispenser to prevent any excess batter from dripping onto the pan.

4 The Roti Jala is cooked once it pulls away from the pan easily (about 3 min). Fold it into quarters then remove. Do not flip it as you would a pancake.

5 Continue with steps 3 and 4, stirring the batter each time (as the flour tends to sink to the bottom).

6 Cover the Roti Jala with cling film or a clean moist tea towel until it is ready to be served.

Curry Devil

Chicken curry with mixed vegetables

Curry Devil, or Curry Debal as it is sometimes known, is a dish of Eurasian origin. It is traditionally served during Christmas and other festive occasions.

The Eurasians, much like the Peranakans, were early settlers in South East Asia. I believe the Eurasians and Peranakans can identify with each other since they are both minority communities with a distinct 'sub-culture', complete with their own patois and cuisine. Over the years, both cultures have increasingly intermarried with the locals, subsequently identifying themselves with the country where they reside rather than as Eurasians or Peranakans.

What is fascinating about Eurasian cuisine is that, much like the Peranakans, there is a liberal use of ingredients from various cultures, seen especially in this delightful dish: roast pork (*char siew*) and rice vinegar from the Chinese; turmeric, candlenuts and prawn paste from the South East Asians; served with a French loaf (baguette), which is evidence of French colonial influence.

INGREDIENTS

1 medium-sized chicken (about 1 kg) or 1 kg chicken pieces
500 g Chinese roast pork (*babi pangang/char siew*)
6 fresh red chillies
6 fresh green chillies
300 g cabbage
15 shallots (*bawang merah*)
6 cloves garlic (*bawang putih*)
1 thumb size knob ginger (*halia*)
1 tbsp mustard power or seeds
1 tbsp Chinese rice vinegar or white vinegar
8 tbsp oil
1 l water
1¹/₂ tbsp sugar
salt, to taste

REMPAH

¹/₂ thumb size knob turmeric (*kunyit*)
40 shallots (*bawang merah*)
20 dried red chillies or 2 tbsp pounded fresh red chillies
6 candlenuts (*buah keras*)
2 tbsp prawn (shrimp) paste (*belacan*)

PREPARATION

1 If dried red chillies are used for the *rempah*, soak them in hot water.
2 If a whole chicken is used, rinse then cut the chicken into pieces.
3 Cut the roast pork into small pieces.
4 Slit the fresh red and green chillies lengthwise then deseed, if preferred.
5 Cut the cabbage into 3 cm squares.
6 Peel and finely slice the shallots, garlic and ginger.
7 Mix the mustard powder or seeds and vinegar together.
8 Prepare the *rempah*. Peel and roughly chop the turmeric and shallots. If dried red chillies are used, drain then roughly chop them (deseed, if preferred). Pound/grind all the *rempah* ingredients together. (See page 192)

METHOD

1 Heat a wok over a high flame until it smokes. Add the oil.
2 Lower the flame. Stir-fry the garlic and shallots until golden brown. Remove and drain.
3 Stir-fry the ginger. Remove and drain.
4 Fry the roast pork for 2–3 min. Remove and drain.
5 Over a high flame, fry the chicken for 3–5 min. Remove and drain.
6 Add more oil if necessary then stir-fry the *rempah* over a high flame for 1 min. Sprinkle in some water to prevent it from burning, then stir-fry over a low flame for 2 min.
7 Over a high fire, add the roast pork and chicken back into the wok.
8 Add the water, chillies, mustard mixture and the fried ingredients.
9 Add the cabbage. Simmer until the chicken is tender (about 30 min).
10 Season with sugar and salt to taste.
11 Serve with slices of French loaf or white rice.

Kurma Chicken

Chicken in a mild creamy curry sauce

INGREDIENTS

1 medium-sized chicken (about
  1 kg) or 1 kg chicken pieces

1 tomato

1 stalk coriander (Chinese
  parsley) (*daun ketumbar*)

1 onion (*bawang*)

4 cloves garlic (*bawang putih*)

12 tbsp oil

$1^1/_2$ tsp salt

MARINADE

150 g ginger (*halia*)

10 tbsp evaporated milk

1 tbsp kalamansi lime (*limau
  kesturi*) or lemon juice

10 tbsp kurma powder

COCONUT MILK

125 g ($^1/_4$) grated coconut

280 ml water

(makes about 350 ml coconut
  milk)

PREPARATION

1 If a whole chicken is used, rinse then cut the chicken into pieces.

2 Peel then pound/grind the ginger for the marinade. Squeeze over a sieve or using a muslin bag to extract $1^1/_2$ tbsp juice.

3 In a large bowl, mix the ginger juice, evaporated milk, lime or lemon juice and kurma powder together, then add the chicken.

4 Rinse then quarter the tomato and roughly chop the coriander.

5 Peel then slice the onion and garlic.

6 Prepare the coconut milk. (See page 193)

METHOD

1 Heat a wok over a high flame until it smokes. Add the oil.

2 Reduce the flame, then stir-fry the onion until light golden brown. Remove.

3 Stir-fry the garlic until light golden brown. Remove.

4 Stir-fry the chicken over a low fire until the oil surfaces.

5 Add the coconut milk and salt.

6 Bring to the boil then simmer uncovered. (Stir continually to prevent the coconut milk from curdling.)

7 Add the tomato, fried onion, fried garlic and coriander.

8 Simmer for 20 min or more until the chicken is cooked.

Peking Duck

Roasted duck marinated in herbs and spices

INGREDIENTS

1 whole duck (about 1.5 kg)

oil, for deep-frying

MARINADE

6 spring onions (scallions)

6 tbsp Chinese cooking wine
   or sherry

2 tbsp light soy sauce

4 thumb size pieces ginger
   (*halia*)

15 cloves (*bunga cengkih*)

4 star anise (*bunga lawang*)

2 tsp cumin (*jintan putih*)

2 tsp fennel (*jintan manis*)

PREPARATION

1 Crush the spring onions then mix with the wine or sherry and light soy sauce. Place the spring onions in the cavity of the duck.

2 Rub the inside and outside of the duck with the remaining wine or sherry and soy sauce mixture. Set the duck aside for 2 hr or freeze for later use.

3 Remove the spring onions and reserve. Peel and slice the ginger. Place half the amount of ginger in the cavity.

4 Add the cloves, star anise, cumin and fennel to the reserved spring onions and remaining ginger then rub the outside of the duck with the marinade.

5 Steam for 1 hr. Remove and drain. Allow to cool and dry.

METHOD

1 Heat a wok over a high flame unit it smokes. Add the oil.

2 When the oil starts to smoke, place the duck in the oil. Turn off the flame.

3 Using a ladle, carefully pour hot oil over parts of the duck not submerged in oil.

4 If the oil is not very hot, turn the flame on again.

5 Continue to ladle hot oil over the duck until the duck is golden brown and even in colour.

6 Remove and drain. Set aside to cool.

7 Chop into smaller pieces then arrange on a large serving plate with the pickles and sauce (see below).

Pickles

Pickled cucumbers, onions and chillies—a simple and basic pickle

INGREDIENTS

1 cucumber

1 onion (*bawang*)

1 fresh red chilli

1 tbsp Chinese rice vinegar
   or white vinegar

2 tsp sugar

1 tsp salt

PREPARATION

1 Peel then halve the cucumber. Remove the seeds and cut into 3 cm strips.

2 Peel and slice the onion into thin strips.

3 Slice the chilli (deseed, if preferred).

METHOD

1 Mix the cucumber and some salt. Set aside for 10 min. Rinse well then squeeze dry using a muslin cloth.

2 Mix the cucumber, onion, chilli, vinegar, sugar and remaining salt together. Serve in a small dish.

Sauce

A salty sauce that is the perfect accompaniment to Peking Duck

INGREDIENTS

1 tbsp salted soy beans
   (*taucheo*)

1 tsp dark soy sauce

1 tsp sesame oil

2 tsp sugar

1 tbsp water

PREPARATION

1 If whole salted soy beans are used, pound the beans.

2 In a small bowl, mix the ingredients together.

METHOD

1 Over a low flame, cook the ingredients together for 10 min.

2 Serve in a small dish.

pork

Tau You Bak

Pork braised in a sweet and salty dark soy sauce

INGREDIENTS

600 g pork belly

6 cloves garlic (*bawang putih*)

2 tbsp oil

6 tbsp sugar

6 tbsp dark soy sauce

280 ml water

Tips:

- This is an extremely easy dish to prepare. The trick is to stir-fry the pork and sugar until the sugar has caramelised and glazed the surface of the pork so that it has a sheen.
- Add shelled hardboiled chicken or quail eggs as an option.
- Steamed Chinese buns (*mantou*) can be served on the side or serve it with steaming hot rice porridge (congee).

PREPARATION

1 Slice the pork belly into thick slices.

2 Peel then mince the garlic.

METHOD

1 Heat a wok over a high flame until it smokes. Add the oil.

2 Add the pork. Seal the meat by frying over a high flame for about 3 min.

3 Lower to a medium flame, then add the garlic and sugar.

4 Stir-fry until the sugar has coated and glazed the pork.

5 Add the dark soy sauce and continue frying for about 2 min.

6 Add the water. Simmer uncovered until the sauce has thickened and the meat is tender, about 30 min or preferably more.

Pork Spareribs

Baby pork ribs grilled and glazed in a tangy sweet soy sauce

INGREDIENTS

900 g small or medium
    pork ribs

MARINADE

4 tbsp Golden syrup or
    Karo syrup

4 tbsp dark soy sauce

3 tbsp light soy sauce

4 tbsp water

1 tsp salt

PREPARATION

1 In a pot, mix the marinade ingredients together. Add the pork ribs. Allow to marinate for 30 min or more.

METHOD

1 Preheat the oven to 200°C.

2 Place the pot on the stove. Bring to the boil then simmer for 15 min before turning the pork ribs over and simmering for another 15 min.

3 Remove then grill for about 5 min on each side until slightly brown and crisp at the edges.

Char Siew

Roast pork with a tangy sweet flavour

INGREDIENTS
900 g pork

MARINADE
$1/2$ tsp dark soy sauce
$1/2$ tsp light soy sauce
$1/2$ tsp orange food colouring
a pinch of yellow food colouring
4 tbsp water
1 tbsp hot water
7 tbsp sugar
$1/2$ tsp salt

Tip:
Char Siew is a versatile meat that can be served with plain rice or used to make Chinese Fried Rice (see page 146).

PREPARATION
1 Slice the pork into strips 3 cm thick.
2 Mix the ingredients for the marinade together. Add the pork then knead together. Set aside for about 2 hr in the refrigerator.

METHOD
1 Preheat the oven to 200°C (ensure that the top grill is on).
2 Place the pork on an oven rack or tray and reserve the marinade for basting. Grill the meat for about 10 min on each side basting with the marinade every 5 min.
3 Increase the heat to 240°C then grill for another few min until the surface is slightly charred.

Sweet and Sour Pork

Crispy deep-fried pork served in a tangy sweet and sour tomato sauce

Sweet and Sour Pork is probably the most ubiquitous dish in Chinatowns all over the world and in Chinese restaurants in Asia. I have sadly tasted my share of badly-made versions: too much MSG, pork that is too fatty and overcooked vegetables.

My best advice is: use good quality pork; fry the pork until crisp but not overcooked and drain well; stir-fry the vegetables quickly and do not overcook; finally, once the sauce has thickened, combine the ingredients together quickly then serve immediately.

INGREDIENTS

700 g pork loin

200 g corn flour (cornstarch)

2 tomatoes

1 onion (*bawang*)

1 cucumber

2 fresh red chillies or 1 red capsicum (bell pepper)

oil, for deep-frying

MARINADE

1 egg

2 tbsp water

$1/2$ tsp bicarbonate of soda

1 tsp sugar

$1/2$ tsp salt

CORN FLOUR MIXTURE

2 tbsp corn flour (cornstarch)

6 tbsp water

GRAVY

280 ml water

8 tbsp tomato sauce or ketchup

3 tbsp Chinese rice vinegar or white vinegar

$1/2$ tbsp Worcestershire sauce

$1/2$ tbsp chilli sauce

1 tsp sesame oil

9 tbsp sugar

1 tsp salt

PREPARATION

1 Cut the pork into bite-sized cubes.

2 Mix the ingredients for the marinade then knead together with the pork. Dust the meat with corn flour.

3 Quarter the tomatoes. Peel and quarter the onion.

4 Rinse, halve lengthwise then deseed the cucumber. Cut into thick slices.

5 Deseed, if preferred, then slice the chillies.

6 Mix the corn flour with the water.

7 Mix the gravy ingredients together.

METHOD

1 Heat a wok over a high flame until it smokes. Add the oil.

2 When the oil is hot, dust off the excess corn flour from the pork then add to oil. Stir-fry until golden brown. Remove and drain.

3 Clean the wok then add $1^1/2$ tbsp oil. Reheat the wok over a high flame.

4 Stir-fry the vegetables for 2 min. Remove then reheat the wok.

5 Add the gravy then bring to the boil. Stir in the corn flour mixture.

6 Bring to the boil. Stir in the vegetables then the pork. Serve immediately.

Tips:

- Sweet and Sour Prawns can be prepared using this same recipe, with the addition of spring onions.

- Sweet and Sour Fish can also be prepared using this recipe, except that the fish is deep-fried whole and the gravy is poured over the fish.

- For a healthier version, use lean pork. For a vegetarian version, substitute the pork with carrots, celery or capsicums (bell peppers).

Sohoon Pork

Glass noodles stir-fried with minced pork and potato cubes

INGREDIENTS

100 g glass noodles (*tunghoon* or *sohoon*)

2 potatoes

1 onion (*bawang*)

5 tbsp oil

160 g minced pork

10 tbsp water

1 tbsp dark soy sauce

2 tsp sugar

$1/4$ tsp salt

$1/4$ tsp pepper

PREPARATION

1 Soak the glass noodles in water.

2 Peel then cube the potatoes. Soak in water to prevent the potatoes from discolouring.

3 Peel then dice the onion.

METHOD

1 Heat a wok over a high flame until it smokes. Add the oil.

2 Thoroughly drain the potatoes then shake off any excess water. Add the potatoes to the oil then fry until light golden brown. Remove and drain. Set aside.

3 Stir-fry the onion until light golden brown.

4 Add the pork then continue frying.

5 Return the fried potatoes to the wok then add small handfuls of glass noodles over the potatoes. Toss the ingredients together.

6 Add 4 tbsp water and dark soy sauce. Toss together to coat the noodles with soy sauce.

7 Add the remaining water, sugar, salt and pepper.

8 Over a medium flame, continue to toss the ingredients together until the noodles are cooked.

Pork Chops

Pork chops marinated and fried in a soy sauce, served with potatoes and tomatoes

This is another dish that probably emerged from the kitchens of Hainanese cookboys during the colonial era. While the inspiration is European, the execution has an Asian twist. The cut of meat used (ie. pork chop) and the inclusion of a potato and tomato is European, while the use of soy sauce, ginger and corn flour is most definitely Chinese. Nevertheless, a tasty and easy dish was created and has become a mainstay of menus in Hainanese restaurants serving Western fare today. Other variations of this dish commonly include onions and/or peas.

INGREDIENTS

300 g pork chops
1 potato
1 tomato
oil, for frying

MARINADE

1 tbsp light soy sauce
$1/2$ tsp dark soy sauce
1 slice ginger (*halia*)
$1/4$ tsp salt

SAUCE

$1/4$ tsp dark soy sauce
1 tsp corn flour (cornstarch)
10 tbsp water
$1/2$ tsp sugar
$1/2$ tsp salt

PREPARATION

1 Tenderise the pork chops with the blunt edge of a cleaver or prick it with a fork.

2 Mix the ingredients for the marinade together, then add the pork. Knead together.

3 Mix the ingredients for the sauce together.

4 Peel and slice the potato.

5 Quarter or slice the tomato.

METHOD

1 Heat a wok over a high flame until it smokes. Add the oil.

2 Fry the potatoes until golden brown. Remove and drain.

3 Reheat the oil then fry the pork chops.

4 Once the pork chops are cooked, drain the excess oil.

5 Add the sauce and potatoes. Bring to the boil then simmer for about 3 min.

Fried Kiam Chai with Pork

Preserved mustard cabbage stir-fried with pork

INGREDIENTS

200 g preserved mustard
  cabbage (*kiam chai*)
80 g pork fat
100 g pork belly
2 cloves garlic (*bawang putih*)
1¹/₂ tbsp sugar
1 tbsp dark soy sauce

Tip:

For a healthier version, use
vegetable oil to fry the garlic, sliced
pork and shredded mustard
cabbage (steps 4 and 5) or omit
the pork fat altogether.

PREPARATION

1 Soak the salted mustard cabbage in water. Remove and discard the water until the mustard cabbage is only slightly salty. Repeat this 2–3 times if necessary. Squeeze dry then shred.

2 Cut the pork fat into small cubes. Slice the pork belly into strips.

3 Peel then mince the garlic.

METHOD

1 Heat a wok over a medium flame.

2 Without any oil, dry-fry the mustard cabbage for 2–3 min. Remove.

3 Over a high flame (with no oil), stir-fry the pork fat until it is crisp and light golden brown. The oil from the fat will be released as it continues to fry. Remove and drain.

4 Return 2 tbsp of the pork fat back into the wok and stir-fry the garlic until light golden brown.

5 Over a high flame, add the sliced pork then the shredded mustard cabbage. Stir-fry for 1 min.

6 Add the sugar and dark soy sauce.

7 Return the crispy fried pork fat cubes to the wok, mix well and serve.

Teehee Char Rebung

Pigs lungs stir-fried with pork and bamboo shoots

It is unlikely that many readers will prepare this dish since lungs are not commonly eaten today, not to mention difficult to obtain and cumbersome to prepare. Even my grandmother mentioned in her cookbook, published in the 1970s, that this recipe had become less popular.

Despite this, I feel it is important that not a single one of my grandmother's recipes be left out of the revised cookbook, no matter how strange or unusual it is. I went through a great deal of trouble trying to locate a pair of fresh pork lungs, only to discover that it is now illegal in Singapore. As a substitute, I used 1 kg of beef lungs and boiled it in water until it was thoroughly cooked (under 1 hr), then proceeded to follow the rest of the recipe. As it turns out, the dish is quite delightful since the meat is soft and tender and the strong flavours of the garlic, ginger and salted soy beans complements it.

INGREDIENTS

1 pair pork or 1 kg beef lungs (*teehee*)

300 g pork belly

300 g cooked bamboo shoots (*rebung*)

10 cloves garlic (*bawang putih*)

1 thumb size knob ginger (*halia*)

2 tbsp salted soy beans (*taucheo*)

5 tbsp oil

8 tbsp water

1 tbsp sugar

1 tsp salt

PREPARATION

1 Prepare the lungs. Place the lungs in a pot of cold water. Bring to the boil. Allow the windpipe to hang over the edge of the pot, so that the foam will drain out while cooking. Skim off the impurities that surface using a spoon/ladle. Once the lungs are cooked, place the pot in running water. Knead the lungs as it soaks in the water. Remove, squeeze dry then slice lungs into strips.

2 Place the pork belly in cold water. Bring to the boil then simmer until cooked. Remove then slice.

3 Drain then shred the bamboo shoots.

4 Peel then pound the garlic. Squeeze dry and discard the juice.

5 Peel then thinly slice the ginger. Rub with salt. Rinse then squeeze dry.

6 If whole salted soy beans are used, pound the beans.

METHOD

1 Heat a wok over a high flame until it smokes. Add the oil.

2 Lower the flame then stir-fry the garlic until light golden brown.

3 Add the ginger then sprinkle in some water to prevent it from burning.

4 Add the salted soy beans. Stir-fry.

5 Add the remaining water, pork belly, bamboo shoots, lungs, sugar and salt.

6 Stir-fry for a few min, then simmer for 5–10 min.

7 Remove and place on a serving plate.

Rebung Char

Bamboo shoots, prawns and pork in a spicy gravy

INGREDIENTS

240 g cooked bamboo shoots
   (*rebung*)

160 g pork

160 g small prawns (shrimps)

280 ml water

1 large dried cuttlefish (*juhee*)

4 cloves garlic (*bawang putih*)

1^1/$_2$ tbsp salted soy beans
   (*taucheo*)

3 tbsp oil

1 tsp sugar

^{1}/$_4$ tsp salt

PREPARATION

1 Drain then shred the bamboo shoots.

2 Rinse then slice the pork into strips or thin slices.

3 Shell and devein the prawns. Set aside the meat. Pound the shells in a mortar and pestle. Add the water to the pounded shells then strain. Keep the stock, discard the shells.

4 Slice then soak the cuttlefish for about 30 min to remove the saltiness and allow it to soften. Leave to soak for longer if necessary.

5 Peel then pound the garlic.

6 If whole salted soy beans are used, pound the beans.

METHOD

1 Heat a wok over a high flame until it smokes. Add the oil.

2 Lower the flame then stir-fry the garlic until light golden brown.

3 Add the salted soy beans and sprinkle in some water (to prevent burning).

4 Add the pork, prawns, cuttlefish and bamboo shoots. Stir-fry for 3–5 min.

5 Add the prawn stock, sugar and salt.

6 Bring to boil then simmer for about 20 min.

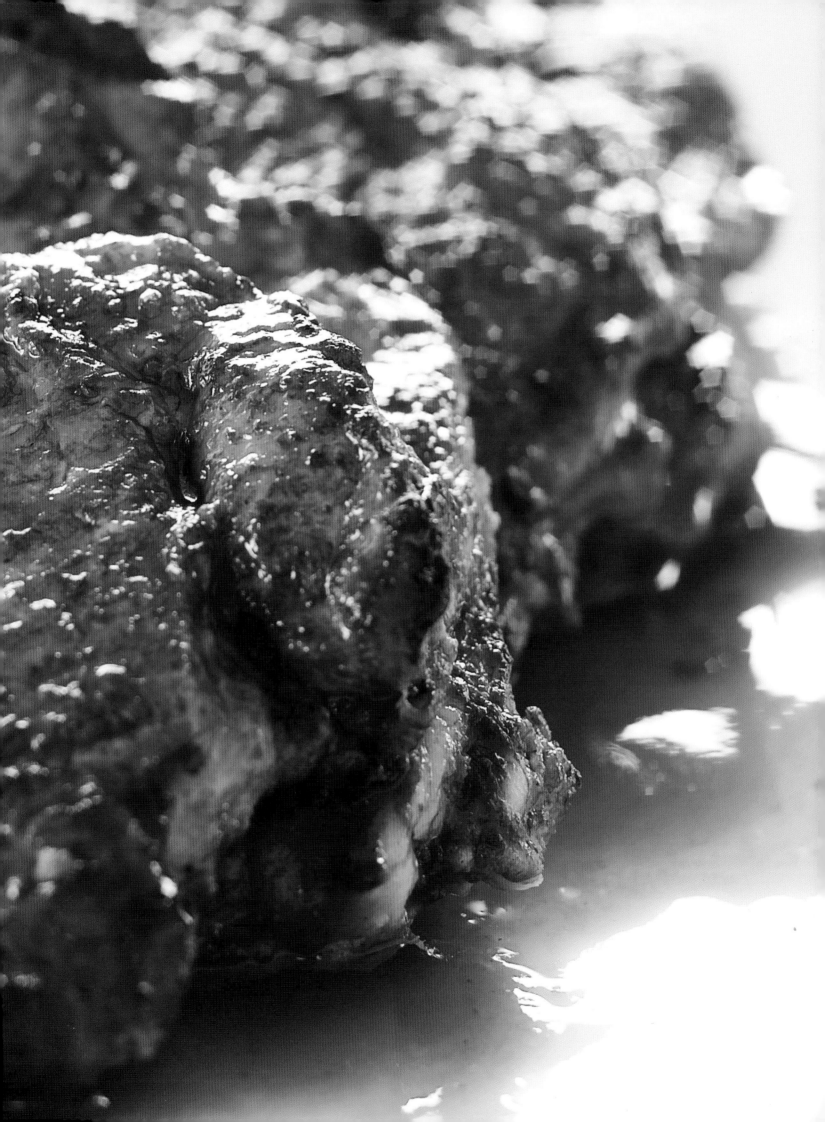

beef and mutton

Beef/Mutton Curry

Beef/mutton stewed in a curry gravy

This a Malay dish that is traditionally served with Nasi Kuning (see page 114), which literally means 'yellow rice'.

INGREDIENTS

1 kg beef or mutton

$^1/_2$ thumb size knob ginger (*halia*)

8 cloves garlic (*bawang putih*)

1 onion (*bawang*)

8 tbsp oil

10 cardamoms (*buah pelaga*)

1 stick cassia bark (*kaya manis*)

8 cloves (*bunga cengkih*)

2 tbsp ketchup

2 tbsp tomato paste

8 tbsp evaporated milk

280 ml water

1 tbsp kalamansi lime (*limau kesturi*) or lemon juice

2 tsp sugar

2 tsp salt

MARINADE

100 g ginger (*halia*)

2 tbsp beef or mutton curry powder

4 tbsp water

1 tsp salt

CURRY PASTE

8 tbsp curry powder

10 tbsp water

PREPARATION

1 Rinse then cut the beef or mutton into pieces.

2 Peel then pound/grind the ginger for the marinade. Squeeze over a sieve or using a muslin bag to extract 1 tbsp juice. In a large bowl, mix the ingredients for the marinade together. Add the meat then marinate for 30 min or more.

3 Peel then pound/grind the ginger and garlic together.

4 Peel then finely slice the onion.

5 Mix the water and curry powder into a paste.

METHOD

1 Heat a wok over a high flame until it smokes. Add the oil.

2 Reduce to a medium flame. Stir-fry the pounded ginger and garlic.

3 Stir-fry the onion then add the curry paste.

4 Sprinkle in some water, then add the cardamom, cassia bark, cloves, ketchup and tomato paste.

5 Add the meat, evaporated milk, 280 ml water and lime or lemon juice.

6 Season with sugar and salt to taste.

7 Simmer for 30 min or more until cooked and tender.

Nasi Kuning

Turmeric-coloured rice garnished with fried shallots, raisins and almonds

This dish of Malay origin always looks impressive at the table, especially for Sunday lunches, dinners or parties. I find that most people love the seasoned rice since it tastes as good as it looks and is the perfect accompaniment to curry. It is also relatively easy to prepare.

INGREDIENTS

600 g Indian long grain rice (Basmati)

2 cloves garlic (*bawang putih*)

1/2 tsp turmeric powder (*kunyit*)

100 ml oil

4 tbsp butter

8 cloves (*bunga cengkih*)

8 cardamoms (*buah pelaga*)

1 stick cassia bark (*kayu manis*)

980 ml water or chicken stock

1 tsp salt

1 chicken stock cube, optional

GARNISHES

8 shallots (*bawang merah*)

100 g raisins

200 g almond flakes

PREPARATION

1 Rinse then drain the rice.

2 Peel then pound the garlic. Mix together with the turmeric powder.

3 Peel then finely slice the shallots.

METHOD

1 Heat a wok or pot over a medium flame. Add the oil.

2 Lightly fry the raisins. Remove and drain.

3 Using the same oil, stir-fry the almonds until light golden brown. Remove and drain. Alternatively, toast the almonds in a toaster oven.

4 Stir-fry the sliced shallots until light golden brown. Remove and drain. Discard the oil and wipe the wok or pot clean.

5 Over a low flame, melt the butter.

6 Stir-fry the garlic and turmeric mixture.

7 Add the cloves, cardamoms, cassia bark then the rice. Stir-fry.

8 Add the water or chicken stock, salt and the chicken stock cube.

9 Bring to the boil then simmer until the rice is cooked and almost dry. Cover and leave to steam for another 5 min over a low flame.

10 Garnish with the fried shallots, raisins and almonds.

Beef Brisket Curry

Beef brisket in a curry gravy

INGREDIENTS

1.5 kg beef brisket

1 onion (*bawang*)

4 cloves garlic (*bawang putih*)

8 tbsp oil

1 tbsp kalamansi lime (*limau kesturi*) or lemon juice

3 tsp sugar

3 tsp salt

CURRY PASTE

10 tbsp Nonya beef curry powder

10 tbsp water

COCONUT MILK

250 g (¹/₂) grated coconut

450 ml water

(makes about 550 ml coconut milk)

TAMARIND MARINADE

¹/₂ rounded tbsp tamarind (*asam*) pulp

10 tbsp water

PREPARATION

1 Cut the beef into cubes.

2 Peel then slice the onion and garlic.

3 Mix the curry powder and water into a paste.

4 Prepare the coconut milk. (See page 193)

5 Prepare the tamarind marinade. (See page 193)

METHOD

1 Heat a wok over a high flame until it smokes. Add the oil.

2 Lower the flame then stir-fry the onion and garlic until golden brown.

3 Sprinkle in a little tamarind marinade.

4 Add the curry paste, stir-fry then add the remaining tamarind marinade.

5 Over a high flame, add the meat. Stir-fry.

6 Add the coconut milk then bring to the boil, stirring continually to prevent it from curdling.

7 Reduce to a medium flame then simmer uncovered until the meat is tender (30 min, preferably more).

8 Add the kalamansi lime or lemon juice. Season with sugar and salt.

Nasi Kunyit

Glutinous rice flavoured with turmeric and coconut cream

In the old days, and perhaps even today, some meticulous Nonyas would separate the glutinous rice grains from the white rice grain by grain, since they are grown close together in the fields and are mixed when harvested. Glutinous rice grains are rounder, shorter, opague and white, while rice grains are longer, thinner, translucent and slightly biege in colour.

INGREDIENTS

1.2 kg glutinous rice (*pulut*)

4 tbsp turmeric (*kunyit*) powder

1 tsp kalamansi lime (*limau kesturi*) or lemon juice

1 tbsp salt

COCONUT CREAM

1 kg (2 whole) grated coconut

water (see Notes below)

(makes about 300 ml coconut cream)

Notes:

- There are two methods that can be used to prepare the coconut cream. In my grandmother's original cookbook, she recommends adding 8 tbsp water then squeezing the grated coconut. This will yield about 300 ml coconut cream, depending on the quality of the grated coconut used and how well you can squeeze it.

- I find another method, which is also commonly used to extract coconut cream, easier. Add sufficient water to soak the grated coconut then extract the coconut milk by squeezing the pulp using a muslin cloth or sieve. Let the coconut milk rest to allow the cream to rise to the surface. Skim it off with a spoon.

PREPARATION

1 Rinse then drain the rice. Repeat this 3 times.

2 Add the turmeric powder and stir well into the rice. Set aside for 10 min.

3 Add enough water to immerse the rice, then set aside overnight or for at least 12 hr.

4 Rinse the rice until the water is clear.

5 Add the lime or lemon juice then rinse until the citrus scent is gone.

6 Prepare the coconut cream. (See page 193)

METHOD

1 Fill a steamer with water then bring the water to the boil.

2 Place the soaked rice into the top tier of the steamer. Create steam holes in the rice by poking the tip of a chopstick all the way down to the bottom of the rice. These steam holes will enable the rice to cook evenly.

3 Steam the rice for 5 min.

4 Stir the rice then steam for another 15–20 min.

5 Place the coconut cream and salt in a pot with a lid.

6 Scoop the steamed rice into the pot, stir thoroughly then cover. Set aside until the rice has absorbed the coconut cream. This will take about 5 min.

7 Place the rice back into the steamer. Steam for another 5 min or until the rice is cooked.

Chilli Beef

Beef stewed then fried in a hot chilli sauce

INGREDIENTS

500 g rump beef

7 tbsp oil

1 tsp Chinese rice vinegar
or white vinegar

1 tsp sugar

$^{1}/_{4}$ tsp salt

SAUCE

1 tsp Chinese rice vinegar
or white vinegar

5 tbsp water

1 tsp sugar

1 tsp salt

REMPAH

15 fresh red chillies

4 shallots (*bawang merah*)

PREPARATION

1 Slice and slightly pound the beef.

2 Prepare the *rempah*. Deseed, if preferred, then roughly chop the chillies. Peel and roughly chop the shallots. Coarsely pound/grind the chillies and shallots together. (See page 192)

METHOD

1 In a pot, combine the beef and the sauce ingredients. Bring to the boil then simmer over a low flame until the sauce has reduced and thickened (30–40 min). Remove and allow to cool then strain.

2 Heat a wok over a high flame until it smokes. Add 2 tbsp oil.

3 Add the cooked beef. Stir-fry until browned on the outside to seal the beef. (This will lock the juices in.) Remove and drain. Discard the oil.

4 In the same wok, add the remaining 5 tbsp oil. Stir-fry the *rempah* for a few min, then add the beef.

5 Add the vinegar, sugar and salt. Stir-fry to mix well for a few min.

6 Remove and place on a serving plate.

Minute Steak

Steak served with gravy

As its name suggests, Minute Steak is a slice of steak cut thinly so that it is cooked within minutes of being fried.

This dish was probably created by resourceful Hainanese cookboys working in the kitchens of wealthy British or Peranakan homes. It is still found on the menus of steak houses in Singapore and Malaysia.

INGREDIENTS
500 g beef steaks, each about 1 cm thick
oil, for frying

MARINADE
2 tbsp Worcestershire sauce
1 tbsp light soy sauce
2 tbsp corn flour (cornstarch)
$1^1/_2$ tsp bicarbonate of soda
$^1/_2$ egg
12 tbsp water
2 tbsp oil
1 tsp sugar
1 tsp salt

GRAVY
$1^1/_2$ tbsp Worcestershire sauce
$1^1/_2$ tbsp ketchup
8 tbsp water
$^1/_2$ tsp sesame oil
$^3/_4$ tsp sugar
a pinch of salt

Tip:
Fillet is the best cut of meat to use for this dish, although any good cut of meat would suffice.

PREPARATION
1 Soak the steaks in water for 1 hr in the refrigerator. Discard the water. Squeeze then pat the steaks dry with a cloth.

2 In a bowl, mix the marinade ingredients together. Add the steaks then knead together.

3 Allow to marinate for 1 hr or more in the refrigerator.

METHOD
1 In a pot, mix the ingredients for the gravy. Bring to the boil then simmer until it has thickened.

2 Heat a wok over a high flame until it smokes. Add the oil.

3 Heat the oil until it starts to smoke. Then drain the oil into a bowl.

4 Sear 1–2 steaks at a time, over the hot greased surface, for about 2 min on each side.

5 Place the meat on a serving plate then pour the hot gravy over the meat. Serve immediately.

Beef with Mixed Vegetables

Stir-fried beef with mixed vegetables

Very delicious and perfect for simple home-style Chinese meals. Typically, plain rice, a soup and perhaps a few other steamed or stir-fried dishes would accompany this dish.

INGREDIENTS

500 g beef (tenderloin or fillet)

8 dried Chinese mushrooms or 6 florets of broccoli

4 slices ginger (*halia*)

6 spring onions (scallions)

10 tbsp oil

MARINADE

100 g ginger (*halia*)

1 tsp dark soy sauce

$1/2$ tsp light soy sauce

$1/2$ tsp bicarbonate of soda

4 tbsp water

1 tsp sugar

1 tsp salt

1 tbsp corn flour (cornstarch)

2 tbsp oil

SEASONING

2 tbsp oil

1 tsp dark soy sauce

1 tbsp Chinese cooking wine or sherry

1 tsp sesame oil

SAUCE

2 tsp oyster sauce

1 tsp light soy sauce

$1/2$ tsp dark soy sauce

1 tbsp Chinese cooking wine or sherry

$1/2$ tsp sesame oil

1 tbsp corn flour (cornstarch)

8 tbsp water

1 tbsp sugar

1 tsp salt

PREPARATION

1 Peel then pound/grind the 100 g ginger. Squeeze over a sieve or using a muslin bag to extract 1 tbsp juice. In a large bowl, mix the ingredients for the marinade, adding the corn flour and oil last.

2 Finely slice the beef. Add to the marinade. Knead together. Set aside.

3 If dried Chinese mushrooms are used, soak them in hot water until softened. Squeeze dry, discard the stems then slice the rest.

4 Peel then finely slice or shred the ginger. Slice the spring onions into 3 cm lengths.

5 In a small bowl, mix the ingredients for the sauce together.

METHOD

1 Heat a wok over a high flame until it smokes. Add 2 tbsp oil.

2 Stir-fry the mushrooms or broccoli, then sprinkle with water to prevent it from burning.

3 Add the dark soy sauce and wine. Stir-fry for 2 min then add the sesame oil. Remove and set aside.

4 Reheat the wok over a high flame then add the remaining 8 tbsp oil. Stir-fry the sliced or shredded ginger then the beef.

5 When the beef is half-cooked, return the mushrooms or broccoli and sauce to the wok.

6 Bring to the boil then turn off the flame.

7 Toss in the sliced spring onions. Serve immediately.

one-dish meals

In the early days of Singapore, this dish was typically sold by roadside hawkers. The precooked ingredients would be assembled in a bowl then hot soup poured over as and when an order was placed. Today, the dish is still served in hawker centres albeit in a cleaner environment.

This homemade version is served with a generous amount of ingredients and has a wonderfully rich pork and prawn based stock. The key to making good Hokkien Mee Soup is in the stock, which means using high quality prawns and pork, and boiling it for longer. Using fresh vegetables and good quality noodles will also help.

Clockwise from left to right: Fresh yellow egg noodles (Hokkien *mee*), fine rice vermicelli (*beehoon*), bean sprouts (*tauge*), water convolvulus (*kangkung*), sliced pork, sliced red chillies in light soy sauce, crisp-fried sliced shallots, prawns, fried cubes of pork fat and prawn and pork soup stock.

Hokkien Mee Soup (Hae Mee)

Egg noodles served in a prawn and pork soup with a variety of garnishes

My grandmother's original version included 300 g pork skin and 1 pork tail, in addition to 300 g pork ribs or meat. I have substituted these ingredients with 600 g pork ribs or pork meat for a healthier dish.

INGREDIENTS

1 kg fresh yellow egg noodles (Hokkien *mee*)

250 g fine rice vermicelli (*beehoon*)

STOCK

600 g pork ribs or pork

4 dried red chillies

600 g medium-sized prawns (shrimps)

3 l cold water

2 tsp sugar

1 tsp salt

1 tsp black peppercorns (*lada hitam*)

2 tsp dark soy sauce

2 tsp light soy sauce

$^1/_4$ tsp bicarbonate of soda, optional

GARNISHES

30 shallots (*bawang merah*)

1–2 fresh red chillies

2 tbsp light soy sauce

200 g pork fat

600 g bean sprouts (*tauge*)

600 g water convolvulus (*kangkung*)

PREPARATION

1 Peel then finely slice the shallots.

2 Deseed, if preferred, then finely slice the chillies. Place them in a small dish with some light soy sauce.

3 Cut the pork fat into small cubes.

4 Remove and discard the caps and roots of the bean sprouts then soak in cold water. Set aside.

5 Prepare the water convolvulus. Cut off and discard the roots then thoroughly rinse. Pluck the leaves together with some stem (to give the dish a crunchy texture). Discard the rest. Soak in cold water. Set aside.

METHOD

1 Heat a wok over a high flame until it smokes. Add the pork fat then dry-fry. (Do not add any oil since the pork fat will release a lot of oil during frying.) Remove once it is crisp and light golden brown, then drain well. Place in a serving bowl.

2 Add the shallots. Stir-fry in batches until light golden brown. Remove and drain well. Place in a serving bowl. (For a healthier version, discard the oil from the pork fat and substitute with vegetable oil.)

3 Reheat the remaining oil over a high flame. Stir-fry the pork ribs or pork and dried red chillies. Remove then place into a large stock pot.

4 Over a high flame, add more oil, if necessary, then stir-fry the prawns until the shells are crisp. Use the edge of a ladle to press the prawn heads and shells to extract the juice.

5 Remove the prawns once cooked then plunge into the cold water. Shell, slice into half lengthwise and devein (optional) then place on a serving plate.

6 Add the fried prawn shells and prawn stock to the large stock pot with the fried chillies and pork.

7 Bring to the boil. Simmer for about 30 min.

8 Add the sugar, salt, black peppercorns, dark soy sauce and light soy sauce to taste.

9 Remove the pork ribs or pork. Slice the meat then place on a serving dish. Return any bones to the stock. Simmer for 1 hr or preferably longer (2–3 hr).

10 Bring some water to the boil then add the bicarbonate of soda before blanching the bean sprouts and then the water convolvulus separately. (The bicarbonate of soda will help the vegetables retain their colour.) Place on serving plates.

11 Blanch the egg noodles and rice vermicelli separately in boiling water. Place on serving plates.

12 Strain the stock into a large serving bowl.

13 In individual bowls, place some egg noodles and rice vermicelli, then add some pork, prawns and other garnishes on top. Pour the stock over the noodles then serve while hot. Alternatively, place each of the cooked ingredients on separate serving dishes for everyone to help themselves.

Fried Hokkien Mee

Fried egg noodles with seafood and pork

INGREDIENTS

300 g pork belly

500 ml cold water

300 g medium-sized prawns (shrimps)

300 g bean sprouts (*tauge*)

6 stalks water convolvulus (*kangkung*)

1/2 tbsp salted soy beans (*taucheo*)

15 cloves garlic (*bawang putih*)

600 g fresh yellow egg noodles (Hokkien *mee*)

6 tbsp oil

salt to taste

GARNISHES

5 sprigs coriander (Chinese parsley) (*daun ketumbar*)

3 spring onions (scallions)

1 fresh red chilli

1 cucumber

4 eggs

PREPARATION

1 Place the pork and cold water in a pot. Bring the water to the boil then simmer for about 10 min until the pork has cooked. Skim off and discard the impurities that rise to the surface using a spoon/ladle. Remove the pork, allow to cool then slice into strips. Reserve the stock.

2 Shell then devein the prawns. Set the meat aside. Place the prawn shells in a mortar and pestle then pound. Add the pork stock then strain. Set the stock aside. Discard the shells.

3 Remove and discard the caps and roots of the bean sprouts then soak in cold water. Set aside.

4 Prepare the water convolvulus. Cut off and discard the roots then thoroughly rinse. Pluck the leaves together with some stem (to give the dish a crunchy texture). Discard the rest.

5 If whole beans are used, pound the salted soy beans.

6 Rinse then pluck off the leafy parts the coriander and slice the spring onions into strips. Deseed then finely slice the chilli into strips. Soak the strips into cold water to cause them to curl. Peel then halve the cucumber. Remove the seeds then shred.

7 Peel then mince the garlic.

METHOD

1 In a bowl, beat the eggs. Add a pinch of salt. Using a flat pan, make several thin omelettes. Set aside to cool, roll then finely slice. Set aside for the garnish.

2 Heat a wok over a high flame until it smokes. Add the oil.

3 Lower the flame then fry the garlic until it is light golden brown. Remove and drain well.

4 Add the salted soy beans, then sprinkle in a little water to prevent it from burning.

5 Add the strips of pork. Stir-fry for 2–3 min, then add the prawns. Continue frying for a few min then add the stock.

6 Bring to the boil. Add the bean sprouts, water convolvulus then noodles. Mix well. Add salt to taste. Do not overcook it or the noodles will be soggy and the vegetables will lose their crunchiness.

7 Place the noodles on a serving plate. Garnish starting with the fried eggs, shredded cucumber, shredded spring onions, finely sliced chilli, coriander, and finally, fried garlic.

8 Serve with a side dish of Sambal Nanas. (See page 134)

Sambal Nanas

A tangy pineapple and cucumber salad traditionally served with Fried Hokkien Mee

INGREDIENTS

1 cucumber

1 small pineapple

REMPAH

4 tbsp dried prawns (shrimps)
(*udang kering*)

2 fresh red chillies

2 tsp (prawn) shrimp paste
(*belacan*)

MARINADE

2 tbsp Chinese rice vinegar
or white vinegar

1 tbsp kalamansi lime (*limau kesturi*) or lemon juice

sugar to taste

salt to taste

Tip:
Do not leave the cucumber and pineapple for too long after cutting, as they will become soggy.

PREPARATION

1 Peel and dice the cucumber and pineapple into small cubes. Place into a large bowl.

2 Wrap the prawn paste in foil then toast in a dry pan or toaster for about 1–2 min on each side. Remove the foil.

3 Prepare the *rempah*. Deseed, if preferred, then roughly chop the chillies. Pound/grind the dried prawns, chillies and toasted prawn paste together. (See page 192)

4 Prepare the marinade. Stir all the ingredients together until the sugar and salt have dissolved.

METHOD

1 Add the mixture to the cucumber and pineapple. Mix thoroughly. Serve immediately.

Plain Mee Char

A vegetarian fried egg noodles dish served in a sweet sauce

INGREDIENTS

2 tomatoes

2 sprigs coriander (Chinese parsley) (*daun ketumbar*)

6 spring onions (scallions)

12 shallots (*bawang merah*)

12 cloves garlic (*bawang putih*)

5 tbsp oil

6–12 bird's eye chillies (*cili padi*)

1¹/₂ tbsp palm sugar (*gula Melaka*)

$^1/_2$ tbsp dark soy sauce

$^1/_2$ tbsp light soy sauce

$^1/_2$ tsp salt

300 g bean sprouts (*tauge*)

600 g fresh yellow egg noodles (Hokkien *mee*)

PREPARATION

1 Slice the tomatoes into wedges.

2 Finely chop the coriander and spring onions.

3 Peel and slice the shallots and garlic.

METHOD

1 Heat a wok over a high flame until it smokes. Add the oil.

2 Lower the flame. Stir-fry the shallots until golden brown. Remove and drain well. Set aside.

3 Stir-fry the garlic until light golden brown.

4 Add the chillies and palm sugar. Sprinkle in some water to prevent it from burning.

5 Add the dark soy sauce, light soy sauce and salt. Stir-fry.

6 Add the bean sprouts, sliced tomatoes and noodles. Stir-fry.

7 Add the spring onions and coriander. Quickly toss together then place on a large serving dish. Garnish with the fried shallots.

Charbeck (Mee Sua)

Fine rice noodles with kidneys, liver and minced pork

This dish is traditionally served for breakfast on birthdays.

INGREDIENTS

1 pair pork kidneys

1 tbsp brandy

160 g pork liver

2 tbsp salted soy beans (*taucheo*)

1/2 thumb size knob ginger (*halia*)

2 tbsp oil

160 g minced pork

700 ml water

1/2 tsp salt

4 bundles fine rice noodles (*mee sua*)

GARNISHES

6 cloves garlic (*bawang putih*)

2 spring onions (scallions)

2 sprigs coriander (Chinese parsley) (*daun ketumbar*)

PREPARATION

1 Prepare the kidneys. Hold the top opening of the kidney under running water for 3 min. Repeat this for each kidney. Cut into half lengthwise. Remove and discard the centre membrane. Cut each kidney into strips. Soak in water for 15 min. Discard the water then pour boiling water over the kidneys. Soak for another 15 min. Discard the water, rinse then drain. Add the brandy. Knead together then drain. Set aside.

2 Rinse then cut the liver into thin slices.

3 If whole salted soy beans are used, pound the beans.

4 Peel then finely shred the ginger and mince the garlic.

5 Finely shred the spring onions and chop the coriander.

METHOD

1 Heat a wok over a high flame until it smokes. Add the oil.

2 Lower the flame then add the garlic. Stir-fry until light golden brown. Remove and drain. Set aside.

3 Stir-fry the ginger then the salted soy beans. Sprinkle in some water to prevent it from burning.

4 Add the minced pork. Continue to stir-fry for 3–5 min.

5 Once the pork is cooked, add the liver and water.

6 Bring to the boil then simmer. Add salt to taste.

7 In another pot, blanch the rice noodles in boiling water for about 2 min. Be careful not to overcook it. Remove and drain.

8 When serving individual portions, place the rice noodles in a bowl then pour the soup over. Garnish with the fried garlic, spring onions and coriander.

Fried Beehoon

Stir-fried rice vermicelli with seafood, pork and vegetables

INGREDIENTS

300 g fine rice vermicelli
(*beehoon*)

160 g pork

160 g pork liver, optional

160 g small prawns (shrimps)

160 g squid (*sotong*)

3 cloves garlic (*bawang putih*)

8 tbsp oil

200 g bean sprouts (*tauge*) or
flowering cabbage (*choy sum*)

GRAVY

1¹/₂ tbsp light soy sauce

1 tbsp dark soy sauce

12 tbsp water

1 tsp sugar

1 tsp salt

CONDIMENTS

pickled green chillies
or 1–2 fresh red chillies

light soy sauce

Lingham's chilli sauce

PREPARATION

1 Blanch the fine rice vermicelli in boiling water for 1–2 min. Remove then drain well.

2 Slice the pork and liver.

3 Shell then devein the prawns.

4 Clean the squid and slice. (See page 12)

5 Peel then mince the garlic.

6 In a small bowl, mix all the gravy ingredients together.

7 Slice the red chillies. Place the pickled green chillies or the sliced red chillies in a small serving dish. Add some light soy sauce. Set aside.

METHOD

1 Heat a wok over a high flame until it smokes. Add the oil.

2 Over a medium flame, stir-fry the garlic until light golden brown.

3 Add the pork, prawns, liver and squid. Stir-fry.

4 Add the gravy mixture. Bring to the boil then simmer until the sauce has thickened slightly.

5 Add the bean sprouts or flowering cabbage then the rice vermicelli.

6 Use chopsticks or tongs (to prevent the vermicelli from breaking) to toss the ingredients together.

7 Serve with chillies in soy sauce and chilli sauce on the side.

Chow Mein

Egg noodles fried to a crisp topped with a seafood, meat and vegetable gravy

INGREDIENTS

500 g dried or fresh egg noodles

$^1/_4$ tsp bicarbonate of soda, optional

500 g spinach or flowering cabbage (*choy sum*)

500 g medium-sized prawns (shrimps)

200 g pork

100 g pork liver

9 tbsp oil

MARINADE

50 g ginger (*halia*)

2 tsp Chinese cooking wine or sherry

2 tsp light soy sauce

2 tsp corn flour (cornstarch)

a dash of pepper

SAUCE

100 g ginger (*halia*) or 1 tsp ginger powder

1 tbsp oyster sauce

2 tbsp light soy sauce

1 tbsp Chinese cooking wine or sherry

1 tbsp sesame oil

450 ml water

1 tbsp sugar

$1^1/_2$ tsp salt

a dash of pepper

CORN FLOUR MIXTURE

3 tbsp corn flour (cornstarch)

10 tbsp water

PREPARATION

1 Blanch the noodles in boiling water. Remove and drain well.

2 Bring some water to the boil then add the bicarbonate of soda before blanching the spinach or flowering cabbage. (The bicarbonate of soda will help the vegetables retain their colour.)

3 Peel then devein the prawns. (Freeze the shells for use in other recipes.)

4 Finely slice the pork and liver.

5 Peel then pound/grind the ginger for the marinade and sauce. Squeeze over a sieve or using a muslin bag to extract 1 tsp juice for the marinade and 2 tsp juice for the sauce.

6 In a bowl, mix the ingredients for the marinade together. Add the slices of pork then mix well together.

7 In a bowl, mix the ingredients for the sauce together. Set aside.

8 Mix the corn flour and water. Set aside.

METHOD

1 Heat a wok over a high flame until it smokes. Add 6 tbsp oil.

2 Fry the noodles for about 3 min on each side. Be careful not to break the noodles. Remove and drain well then place on a serving plate.

3 Reheat the wok over a high flame. Add the remaining 3 tbsp oil.

4 Stir-fry the marinated pork with the marinade then add the sauce.

5 Stir the corn flour mixture then pour half in. Bring to the boil.

6 Add the prawns and liver. Cook for 2 min.

7 Spread the cooked meat and blanched vegetables over the noodles.

8 Add the rest of the corn flour mixture to the remaining sauce. Bring to the boil.

9 Pour the sauce over the meat and vegetables.

10 Serve immediately while the noodles are still crisp.

Cantonese-Style Fried Noodles

Thin egg noodles stir-fried with meat and vegetables

INGREDIENTS

100 g pork
4 dried Chinese mushrooms
150 g bean sprouts (*tauge*)
   or cabbage
3 spring onions (scallions)
1 onion (*bawang*)
2 cloves garlic (*bawang putih*)
500 g dried or fresh egg noodles
2 eggs
oil, for frying
100 g crab meat

SAUCE

2 tsp Worcestershire sauce
1 tsp dark soy sauce
2 tsp light soy sauce
1 tsp sesame oil
280 ml water
2 tsp sugar
a dash of pepper

GARNISH

1 head local lettuce (*sayur salad*), optional

PREPARATION

1 Slice the pork into thin strips.

2 Soak the Chinese mushrooms in hot water to soften. Squeeze dry. Discard the stems then slice the rest.

3 If bean sprouts are used, remove and discard the caps and roots then soak in cold water. If cabbage is used, shred into thin strips.

4 Shred the lettuce and spring onions.

5 Peel then slice the onion and mince the garlic.

6 If dried noodles are use, soak the noodles in water for about 5 min then drain well.

7 Beat the eggs.

8 Mix the sauce ingredients.

METHOD

Preparing the noodles

1 Heat a wok over a high flame until it smokes. Add the oil.

2 Once the oil starts to smoke, drain off the oil. Lower the flame.

3 Gently pull the noodles apart then spread half the noodles on the wok. Allow it to fry for 30 sec then add 4 tbsp oil.

4 Lift the noodles and turn it over. Fry the other side for half a min. Pour half of the beaten egg over the noodles, then scramble it together with a pair of chopsticks. Remove the fried noodles and set it aside.

5 Repeat the process with the remaining noodles.

Cooking the noodles

1 Heat a wok over a high flame until it smokes. Add the oil.

2 Reduce to a medium flame. Stir-fry the onion and garlic until slightly brown.

3 Add the pork and mushrooms. Stir-fry.

4 Add the spring onions, bean sprouts or cabbage and crab meat. Stir-fry.

5 Add the sauce. Bring to the boil.

6 Add the noodles. Using chopsticks, toss the noodles until the sauce is dry.

7 Place on a large serving plate. Garnish with shredded lettuce.

Chinese Fried Rice

Rice fried with prawns, pork, eggs and vegetables

Prepare this dish using day-old rice for the best results. Avoid using freshly cooked rice as it is moist which will cause the rice to clump together. This dish is often a big hit with kids and it is also good for simple lunches at home.

INGREDIENTS

600 g cold cooked Thai long
   grain rice

500 g prawns (shrimps)

200 g roast pork (*char siew*)
   (see page 96)

6 eggs

10 tbsp oil

SEASONING

$^1/_2$ tbsp light soy sauce

$^1/_2$ tbsp water

$^1/_2$ tsp sugar

$^1/_2$ tbsp salt

GARNISH

6 spring onions (scallions)

PREPARATION

1 Using your fingers, break up any lumps in the rice.

2 Shell, devein then dice the prawns. (Reserve the shells for use in other recipes.)

3 Dice the roast pork so that it is similar in size to the prawns.

4 Beat the eggs.

5 Rinse then finely dice the spring onions.

6 Mix the ingredients for the seasoning together.

METHOD

1 Heat a wok over a high flame until it smokes. Add the oil.

2 Stir-fry the pork and prawns then add the seasoning.

3 Lower to a medium flame then add the rice.

4 Create a crater in the rice then add the beaten eggs. Stir-fry to scramble the eggs, then quickly toss the ingredients together.

5 Serve on a large serving plate. Garnish with sliced spring onions.

Tips:
- To reduce the amount of oil required to fry rice, use a non-stick pan.
- Substitute some of the cooking oil with sesame oil for a subtle sesame flavour.

Kai Chok

Cantonese-style chicken porridge

INGREDIENTS

300 g rice

$^1/_2$ tsp bicarbonate of soda

1 tbsp oil

1 small chicken (600–800 g)

4.5 l water

1–2 chicken stock cubes,
  optional

1 tbsp light soy sauce

1 tbsp salt

GARNISHES

fried shallots (*bawang goreng*)

coriander (Chinese parsley)
  (*daun ketumbar*)

> **Tip:**
>
> For more variety, boil the chicken stock with onions and peppercorns. This dish can also be cooked using minced pork, minced beef or slices of fish.

PREPARATION

1 Rinse the rice. Repeat this 2–3 times.

2 Add the bicarbonate of soda and oil.

METHOD

1 In a large pot, place the chicken in the cold water.

2 Bring to the boil then simmer for 30 min. Skim off and discard the impurities that rise to the surface with a spoon/ladle.

3 Remove and plunge the chicken into cold water to stop the cooking process.

4 Using your fingers, shred the chicken. Return the bones to the stock, then place the shredded chicken on a serving plate.

5 Simmer the stock for another 30 min then strain. Discard the bones.

6 Add the rice, chicken stock cubes, light soy sauce and salt to the stock. Simmer for another 30 min.

7 Serve the porridge in a large bowl with the shredded chicken, fried shallots and coriander in small serving dishes on the side. Alternatively, serve in individual serving bowls.

Macaroni and Chicken Soup

Macaroni served in a chicken broth with garnishes

My grandmother's recipe included the use of chicken stock cubes to enhance the flavour of this dish. I believe they can be omitted since the natural flavour of the chicken stock is sufficient.

INGREDIENTS

4 slices white bread

20 shallots (*bawang merah*)

4 sprigs coriander (Chinese parsley) (*daun ketumbar*)

oil, for frying

4 l cold water

1 medium-sized chicken (about 1 kg)

$1/2$ tsp black peppercorns (*lada hitam*)

1 tsp sugar

1 tsp salt

300 g macaroni

PREPARATION

1 Slice off the crust then cube the bread.

2 Peel and finely slice the shallots.

3 Rinse then pluck off the coriander leaves.

METHOD

1 Heat a wok over a high flame until it smokes. Add the oil.

2 Prepare the croutons. Fry the bread until light golden brown. Remove and drain well. Set aside.

3 Fry the shallots until light golden brown. Remove and drain well. Set aside.

4 Fill a large pot with the cold water. Add the chicken and black peppercorns.

5 Bring to the boil then simmer for 30–40 min. Skim off and discard the impurities that rise to the surface with a spoon/ladle.

6 Remove the chicken then place it in a bowl of cold water to stop the cooking process.

7 Using your fingers, shred the chicken. Return the bones to the stock, then place the shredded chicken on a serving plate.

8 Continue to simmer the stock for another 30 min. Season the stock with sugar and salt to taste.

9 Pass the stock through a sieve.

10 Cook the macaroni in a separate pot of boiling water with a pinch of salt for about 5 min. Plunge into cold water to stop the cooking process then drain.

11 Serve in individual bowls by placing the macaroni then shredded chicken, croutons, fried shallots and coriander into the bowl, then pouring the stock over. Alternatively, serve the ingredients on separate serving plates and the stock in a large soup bowl for everyone to help themselves.

multiple-dish meal

Curry Tiffin

This collection of recipes reflect an era of my grandmother's life. In her 60s and 70s, she used to occupy her time by teaching cooking to expatriate wives, including the wives of the diplomatic corps and British and Australian officers. To suit their Western palates, she taught them a simplified version of Asian cuisine, including her version of Curry Tiffin recipes.

Curry Tiffin originates from India during the British colonial days when the British officers would have various curries, rice and condiments brought to them at the office in tiffin carriers for lunch. The dishes have an Anglo-Indian twist and tend to be less spicy.

An elaborate spread of Curry Tiffin dishes is still available at the famous Tiffin Room at the Raffles Hotel in Singapore, complete with its waiters in white suits, quaint twirling ceiling fans, silverware and starch-ironed linens (see Useful Contacts on page 198).

The accompaniments served with Curry Tiffin are traditionally as numerous as the dishes themselves. Suggested accompaniments for Curry Tiffin include pappadams and 8 condiments (on the tray: sliced bananas, chopped chillies and cucumber, roasted peanuts, chopped boiled preserved duck eggs, mango chutney, fried anchovies (*ikan bilis*), chopped tomatoes and toasted grated coconut.)

Main Curry Tiffin dishes (clockwise from left to right): Fish Moolie, Chicken Curry (Simplified), Udang Goreng Cili, Sayur Lodeh (Simplified), Beef Rendang (Simplified), Achar (Simplified), Chicken Moolie (on the plate with rice) and Egg Sambal.

Other suggested dishes are Satay with satay sauce and its condiments (see pages 40–43).

Fried Curried Chicken

A mild chicken curry

This curry is drier and milder than Nonya Chicken Curry (see page 82) since it uses less curry powder, shallots, garlic and ginger, although the recipe is essentially the same.

INGREDIENTS

1 medium-sized chicken (about 1 kg) or 1 kg chicken pieces

1 onion (*bawang*)

5 tbsp Nonya chicken curry powder

10 tbsp oil

2 tsp salt

REMPAH

2 shallots (*bawang merah*)

2 cloves garlic (*bawang putih*)

2 slices ginger (*halia*) or $^1/_4$ tsp ginger powder

COCONUT MILK

250 g ($^1/_2$) grated coconut

450 ml water

(makes about 550 ml coconut milk)

> **Tips:**
> - For a healthier version of this dish, substitute the coconut milk with evaporated milk.
> - Do not use a cast iron wok since it will make the gravy dark instead of golden yellow.

PREPARATION

1 If a whole chicken is used, rinse then cut the chicken into pieces.

2 Peel then finely slice the onion.

3 Prepare the *rempah*. Peel then roughly chop the shallots, garlic and ginger. Pound/grind the *rempah* ingredients together. (See page 192)

4 Mix the *rempah* and curry powder together then marinate the chicken for at least 1 hr in the refrigerator.

5 Prepare the coconut milk. (See page 193)

METHOD

1 Heat an aluminium or enamel pot or wok over a high flame. Add the oil.

2 Reduce the flame then stir-fry the onion until softened and light golden brown.

3 Over a high flame, add about 5 tbsp coconut milk and the chicken with the marinade.

4 Stir-fry for 1 min, then reduce to a medium flame.

5 Add the remaining coconut milk. Bring to the boil then simmer uncovered until the chicken is tender (20–30 min).

6 Add salt to taste.

Beef Rendang (Simplified)

Stewed beef in a spicy thick sauce

INGREDIENTS

750 g beef (rump or fillet)

1 onion (*bawang*)

4 cloves garlic (*bawang putih*)

$1/2$ thumb size knob ginger (*halia*)
or $1/2$ tsp ginger powder

1 stalk lemon grass (*serai*) or
the peel from $1/4$ lemon or
1 medium-sized lime

1 tbsp coriander (*ketumbar*)
powder

$1/2$ tsp cumin (*jintan putih*)
powder

$1^1/2$ tbsp chilli powder

$3/4$ tbsp sugar

$1/2$ tbsp salt

COCONUT MILK

500 g (1 whole) grated coconut

280 ml water

(makes about 500 ml coconut
milk)

PREPARATION

1 Cut the meat into big or medium cubes, depending on your preference.

2 Peel then slice the onion and mince the garlic.

3 If fresh ginger is used, peel then mince the ginger.

4 If lemon grass is used, peel off the outer layer then bruise (use white portion only).

5 Prepare the coconut milk. (See page 193)

METHOD

1 In a wok or large pot, combine all the ingredients.

2 Bring to the boil then simmer uncovered until the meat is tender and the gravy has reduced to a thick consistency (about 40 min). It is preferable to simmer it for longer (up to 3 hr), in which case, it should be covered. Stir occasionally to prevent the spices from settling at the bottom. Add more water if the gravy reduces too much.

Chicken Moolie

A mild and simple chicken curry

INGREDIENTS

1 medium-sized chicken (about 1 kg) or 1 kg chicken pieces

1 tomato

5 tbsp oil

1 tbsp sugar

1 tbsp salt

REMPAH

$^1/_2$ thumb size knob ginger (*halia*)

12 shallots (*bawang merah*)

2 tsp turmeric (*kunyit*) powder

2 tsp coriander (*ketumbar*) powder

$^1/_2$ tsp cumin (*jintan putih*) powder

2 tbsp chilli powder

COCONUT MILK

500 g (1 whole) grated coconut

850 ml water

(makes about 1 l coconut milk)

PREPARATION

1 If a whole chicken is used, rinse then cut the chicken into pieces.

2 Quarter the tomato.

3 Prepare the *rempah*. Peel and roughly chop the ginger and shallots. Pound/grind all the *rempah* ingredients together. (See page 192)

4 Prepare the coconut milk. (See page 193)

METHOD

1 Heat a wok over a high flame until it smokes. Add the oil.

2 Stir-fry the *rempah* until it is fragrant (about 3 min).

3 Add about 5 tbsp coconut milk. Simmer for 1 min.

4 Over a high flame, add the remaining coconut milk. Bring to the boil while stirring continuously (to prevent the coconut milk from splitting).

5 Add the chicken then reduce to a simmer. Cook for about 10 min.

6 Add the tomato, sugar and salt. Simmer for another 3–5 min.

Fish Moolie

A mild and simple fish curry

INGREDIENTS

500 g fish

1 tomato

5 tbsp oil

$^1/_2$ tbsp sugar

$^1/_2$ tbsp salt

REMPAH

$^1/_2$ thumb size knob ginger
   (*halia*)

12 shallots (*bawang merah*)

1 tsp turmeric (*kunyit*) powder

1 tsp coriander (*ketumbar*)
   powder

$^1/_4$ tsp cumin (*jintan putih*)
   powder

$^1/_2$ tbsp chilli powder

COCONUT MILK

500 g (1 whole) grated coconut

580 ml water

(makes about 750 ml coconut
   milk)

> **Tip:**
> Any meaty white fish such as
> Spanish mackerel (*ikan tenggiri*) or
> red snapper (*ikan merah*) will do.

PREPARATION

1 Rinse then cut the fish into pieces.

2 Quarter the tomato.

3 Prepare the *rempah*. Peel and roughly chop the ginger and shallots. Pound/grind all the *rempah* ingredients together. (See page 192)

4 Prepare the coconut milk. (See page 193)

METHOD

1 Heat a wok over a high flame until it smokes. Add the oil.

2 Stir-fry the *rempah* until it is fragrant (about 3 min).

3 Add about 5 tbsp coconut milk. Simmer for 1 min.

4 Over a high flame, add the remaining coconut milk. Bring to the boil while stirring continuously (to prevent the coconut milk from splitting).

5 Add the fish then reduce to a simmer. Cook for 5 min.

6 Add the tomato, sugar and salt. Simmer for another 3–5 min.

Udang Goreng Cili

Prawns fried with chillies

INGREDIENTS

15 dried red chillies or 2 fresh
  red chillies

300 g medium-sized prawns
  (shrimps)

1 onion (*bawang*)

4 tbsp oil

2 tsp sugar

1 tsp salt

TAMARIND MARINADE

1 rounded tbsp tamarind (*asam*)
  pulp

10 tbsp water

PREPARATION

1 If dried red chillies are used, soak them in hot water to soften. Drain then deseed, if preferred, and pound. If fresh chillies are used, deseed if preferred, then pound.

2 Shell then devein the prawns. (Freeze the shells for use in other recipes.)

3 Peel and slice the onion.

4 Prepare the tamarind marinade. (See page 193)

METHOD

1 Heat a work over a high flame until it smokes. Add the oil.

2 Lower the flame then stir-fry the chillies and onion.

3 Over a high flame, add the prawns. Stir-fry for 1 min.

4 Add the tamarind marinade, sugar and salt.

5 Bring to the boil then simmer uncovered for about 3 min.

Sayur Lodeh (Simplified)

Vegetables stewed in a coconut gravy

This is a simplified version of traditional Sayur Lodeh. It was adapted by my grandmother to suit Western taste buds and bearing in mind the availability of ingredients outside Asia.

INGREDIENTS

200 g small prawns (shrimps)

100 g cooked bamboo shoots (*rebung*) or turnip (*bang kuang*)

100 g cabbage

100 g French beans

100 g long beans (*kacang panjang*)

1 green capsicum (bell pepper)

1 red capsicum (bell pepper)

1 carrot

1 local eggplant (aubergine/ brinjal)

4 cloves garlic (*bawang putih*)

10 shallots (*bawang merah*)

1 tsp chilli powder

water

5 tbsp oil

1 tbsp sugar

1 tsp salt

COCONUT MILK

250 g (¹/₂) grated coconut

670 ml water

(makes about 750 ml coconut milk)

PREPARATION

1 Shell then devein the prawns. (Freeze the shells for use in other recipes.)

2 Slice the bamboo shoots or turnip into small pieces.

3 Cut the cabbage into 3 cm squares.

4 Cut the French beans and long beans into 3 cm lengths.

5 Slice the green and red capsicum into 3 cm squares.

6 Peel then slice the carrot.

7 Cut the eggplant into cubes or thick slices then soak in water (to prevent discolouring).

8 Peel then thinly slice the garlic and shallots.

9 Mix the chilli powder with a little water to form a paste.

10 Prepare the coconut milk. (See page 193)

METHOD

1 Heat a wok over a high flame until it smokes. Add the oil.

2 Reduce to lower flame. Stir-fry the garlic and shallots.

3 Add the chilli paste. Stir-fry for a few seconds.

4 Add the capsicum and prawns. Stir-fry then add the coconut milk.

5 Add the remaining vegetables. Mix well together then add the remaining coconut milk.

6 Bring to the boil then simmer uncovered for about 15 min until the vegetables have softened. Add the sugar and salt.

Tip:

For a healthier version of this dish, substitute the coconut milk with 10 tbsp evaporated milk.

Egg Sambal

Hardboiled eggs in a spicy tomato-based sauce

INGREDIENTS

30 quail eggs or 10 chicken eggs

5 tbsp oil

5 tbsp tomato paste

1 tsp kalamansi lime (*limau kesturi*) or lemon juice

3 tsp sugar

1 tsp salt

REMPAH

1 slice ginger (*halia*)

12 shallots (*bawang merah*)

1 clove garlic (*bawang putih*)

1 tsp chilli powder

COCONUT MILK

125 g (¼) grated coconut

120 ml water

(makes about 200 ml coconut milk)

PREPARATION

1 In a large pot, hardboil then shell the eggs.

2 Prepare the *rempah*. Peel and roughly chop the ginger, shallots and garlic. Pound/ grind all the *rempah* ingredients together. (See page 192)

3 Prepare the coconut milk. (See page 193)

METHOD

1 Heat a wok over a high flame until it smokes. Add the oil.

2 Stir-fry the *rempah* for 1 min then add the tomato paste and stir-fry for another 1 min.

3 Add the eggs and stir-fry for 1 min then add the coconut milk. The sauce will turn a creamy pink.

4 Simmer for a few min before adding the lime or lemon juice, sugar and salt.

5 Continue to simmer for another 3–5 min until the gravy has reduced and turned thick and red.

Achar (Simplified)

Pickled vegetables

INGREDIENTS

1 kg cucumbers
1 tbsp salt
1 carrot
1 onion (*bawang*)
1 fresh red chilli
.1 tbsp sugar
1 tsp salt
3 tbsp oil
4 tbsp Chinese rice vinegar
    or white vinegar

REMPAH

2 candlenuts (*buah keras*)
4 tbsp water
1 tsp turmeric (*kunyit*)

PREPARATION

1 Rinse, halve then deseed the cucumbers. Cut into 3 cm strips.

2 Add the salt to the cucumbers. Set aside for 1 hr. Rinse then squeeze the excess water using a muslin cloth or bag.

3 Peel then cut the carrot into 3 cm strips.

4 Peel then cut the onion into thin slices.

5 Deseed, if preferred, then slice the chilli into thin strips.

6 Mix cucumbers, carrot, onion and chilli. Season with sugar and salt to taste.

7 Prepare the *rempah*. Pound the candlenuts. Add 1 tsp water to the turmeric powder to form a paste. Mix together. (See page 192)

METHOD

1 Heat a wok a medium flame. Add the oil.

2 Stir-fry the candlenuts and turmeric paste for 1 min.

3 Add the vinegar and remaining water then turn off the flame.

4 Allow to cool then add the cucumbers, carrot, onion and chillies.

5 Store in a clean airtight glass jar or set aside for at least 30 min for the flavours to infuse before serving.

Glossary

SPICES & HERBS

1. Coriander Seeds
(*Ketumbar*)
These tiny, round, light brown pods release a strong and distinctive aroma. They are a key ingredient in Peranakan cuisine, in such dishes as Ayam Siow and Hati Babi. They are often sold whole or powdered.

Substitute: (1A) Coriander Powder

2. Cumin Seeds
(*Jintan Putih*)
These tiny, long, dark brown seeds release a musty, woody aroma and are a key spice in Peranakan and South Asian cuisine, particularly in curries. They are often sold whole or powdered in small bottles at the supermarket, or in small packets by spice sellers at the wet market. To prepare your own powder, dry-roast the seeds then pound them until very fine.

Substitute: (2A) Cumin Powder

3. Fennel Seeds
(*Jintan Manis*)
These seeds are typically used in a powdered form in *rempahs*. They have a delicate liquorice, lemony aroma. Although very similar in appearance to cumin seeds, fennel seeds are slightly larger and lighter brown in colour. Often sold whole or powdered in small bottles at the supermarket, or in small packets by the spice seller at the wet market. To prepare your own powder, dry-roast the seeds then pound them until very fine.

Substitute: (3A) Fennel Powder

4. Dried Chillies
Dried red chillies are used for their earthy deep red colour. Remove the stems (if any) then soak in hot water to soften before using. Deseed if you prefer your dish less spicy. One way is to slit the chilli then shake the seeds out before soaking, although not all will fall out. Alternatively, soak in hot or warm water to soften then slice in half and scrap the seeds away using the edge of a sharp knife, as you would a fresh chilli.

Substitutes: (5) Chilli Flakes or (6) Chilli Powder

5. Chilli Flakes
These are coarsely minced dried chillies. They are often fried in oil to obtain chilli oil in recipes such as Laksa.

6. Chilli Powder
This is the powdered version of dried chillies. Chilli powder is used in dishes where the chilli needs to be completely dissolved into the gravy.

7. Black Peppercorns
(*Lada Hitam*)
These small, round dried berries were once worth their weight in gold. Whole peppercorns are particularly good for simmering in stocks since they will slowly release their aroma and flavour.

Substitute: Black Pepper Powder

8. Cardamom
(*Buah Pelaga*)
These oval pods have soft pale green fibrous shells that contain 15–20 tiny black seeds. Cardamom has a refreshing and distinctive lemony aroma. Typically used whole in curries.

Substitute: Cardamom Powder

9. Mixed/Five-spice Powder
A mixture of ground cinnamon, cloves, fennel, star anise and Sichuan peppercorns. Prepare your own using equal quantities of these five spices if it is not available at your local store.

1. Coriander Seeds (*Ketumbar*)

1A. Coriander Powder

4. Dried Chillies

2. Cumin Seeds (*Jintan Putih*)

5. Chilli Flakes

6. Chilli Powder

2A. Cumin Powder

7. Black Peppercorns (*Lada Hitam*)

8. Cardamom (*Buah Pelaga*)

3. Fennel Seeds (*Jintan Manis*)

3A. Fennel Powder

9. Mixed/Five-spice Powder

SPICES & HERBS
(continued)

10. Nutmeg
(*Buah Pala*)
This small, oval, brown seed has a strong and distinctive taste. As such it is always used in small grated amounts to season curries and other dishes. It is not widely used in Peranakan cuisine.

Substitute: (10A) Nutmeg Powder

11. Cassia Bark
(*Kayu Manis*)
Cassia is often mistaken for cinnamon because they are very similar. Cassia releases an aromatic scent and woody flavour when used in curries or stews. Remember to remove it before serving.

Substitutes: (12) Cinnamon Sticks or (12A) Cinnamon Powder

12. Cinnamon Sticks
Although similar in aroma and texture to cassia, cinnamon sticks are slightly thicker and typically have a straighter edge. Use cinnamon sticks in the same way you would use cassia. Remove it before serving.

Substitute: (12A) Cinnamon Powder

13. Star Anise
(*Bunga Lawang/Pekek*)
Also known as star aniseed, this eight-pointed star-shaped spice is widely used in Asian cuisine and is usually added to curries and stocks whole. It releases a strong woody aroma that goes well with meat dishes.

14. Candlenuts
(*Buah Keras*)
The Malay name of this waxy, cream-coloured nut literally translates into 'hard fruit'. They are pounded in *rempahs* and used as a natural thickening agent. They store well for months in a clean airtight container or even better in the freezer (since it can go rancid).

Substitutes: Any skinned fatty white nuts such as macadamias, almonds, hazelnuts or Brazil nuts

15. Ginger
(*Halia*)
This rhizome has a light brown skin and yellow flesh. Use mature ginger in *rempahs* and young ginger for pickling. Peel away the skin before using it sliced, pounded or for its juice. Traditionally measured by slices or thumb size (1 thumb size is equivalent to 5 cm).

Substitute: (15A) Ginger Powder

16. Galangal
(*Lengkuas*)
More commonly known as blue ginger, this rhizome has brownish-pink skin and pale yellow flesh. It is a key ingredient in Peranakan cuisine which gives the cuisine its underlying flavour and aroma. Its flavour is less pungent and more aromatic than ginger, so do not substitute with ginger. Peel away the skin before using. Traditionally measured by slices or thumb size (1 thumb size is equivalent to 5 cm).

Substitute: (16A) Galangal Powder

17. Turmeric
(*Kunyit*)
The vibrant yellow-orange colour and distinctive taste of this rhizome adds colour and enhances the flavour of dishes even when used in small amounts. Be careful when handling it as it stains. Peel away the skin before using. Traditionally measured by slices or thumb size (1 thumb size is equivalent to 5 cm).

Substitute: (17A) Turmeric Powder

10. Nutmeg (*Buah Pala*)

13. Star Anise (*Bunga Lawang/Pekek*)

16. Galangal (*Lengkuas*)

10A. Nutmeg Powder

14. Candlenuts (*Buah Keras*)

16. Galangal Powder

11. Cassia Bark (*Kayu Manis*)

12. Cinnamon Sticks

15. Ginger (*Halia*)

17. Turmeric (*Kunyit*)

12A. Cinnamon Powder

15A. Ginger Powder

17A. Turmeric Powder

SPICES & HERBS
(continued)

18. Lemon Grass
(*Serai*)
To release the refreshing lemony aroma of this long, pale green, fibrous herb, peel away the outer layer of leaves then bruise or slice. Use only the fragrant white bulbous portion and discard the green upper stalk. If it is added whole, remove before serving.

Substitutes: (18A) Lemon Grass Powder or Lemon Peel

19. Coriander
(*Daun Ketumbar*)
Known also as Chinese parsley and cilantro, the leafy parts of this herb are often used as a garnish, although the stem can also be chopped up and used.

20. Chillies
Chillies come in a vast variety of sizes and have varying degrees of intensity. It is a key ingredient in some of the world's most ancient and popular cuisines, spanning South America to South India. The Malay language sensibly differentiates between 'chilly hot' and 'temperate hot' by referring to it as *pedas* and *panas,* respectively.

20A. Fresh Red Chillies
These are ripened chillies and are most commonly used in Asian and Peranakan cuisine, particularly in the preparation of *rempahs*. They are used for their fiery red colour and to intensify the flavour of dishes. The 'heat' comes from the seeds, so adjust the intensity by deseeding the chillies accordingly.

To deseed a chilli, slice in half then scrape the seeds away using the edge of a sharp knife. Avoid touching the seeds when preparing chillies and do not touch your eyes. Chillies can leave a burning sensation on skin. Plunge your hands into cold water to numb the pain.

Substitute: (5) Chilli Flakes or (6) Chilli Powder

20B. Fresh Green Chillies
These are unripened chillies used mostly as a garnish because of its vibrant green colour. Pickled green chillies are also enjoyed for their mild flavour and are often eaten together with noodles by the Chinese in Singapore.

20C. Bird's Eye Chillies
(*Cili Padi*)
As a rule of thumb, the smaller the chilli, the more intense the heat. This chilli is certainly much spicier than regular red chillies. (*Cili padi* is also a colloquial term of endearment for someone who has a fiery personality!)

21. Shallots
(*Bawang Merah*)
These small red bulbs are often referred to as shallots but they are different from their Western counterparts. The local name for these are *bawang merah*, which helps to eliminate the confusion. It has a sweeter and more aromatic aroma than white onions or Western shallots, and is a key ingredient in Peranakan cuisine.

Typically used pounded in *rempahs,* or sliced and fried (*bawang goreng*) for garnish. Soaking makes it easier to remove the thin skin. Peel away from the eyes to avoid tearing.

Substitute: Red or White Onions

22. Kalamansi Lime
(*Limau Kesturi*)
Smaller and deeper green in colour than ordinary lime, kalamansi limes are often used as a garnish served whole or halved. The rind is also used for its citrus flavour and aroma. It is also used for its juice which is golden yellow in colour and sharp and aromatic. Its juice adds sourness to dishes, which helps to whet the appetite.

To make a refreshing drink, squeeze the juice of several kalamansi limes, add cold water and crushed ice, then sweeten with sugar syrup.

Substitutes: Lime or Lemon Juice

23. Fresh Tamarind
(*Asam*)
Fresh tamarind comes in a long brown pod. It has a mild flavour compared to preserved tamarind, so use more if necessary. It keeps best in the refrigerator for a few weeks.

Substitute: (76) Preserved Tamarind (*Asam*)

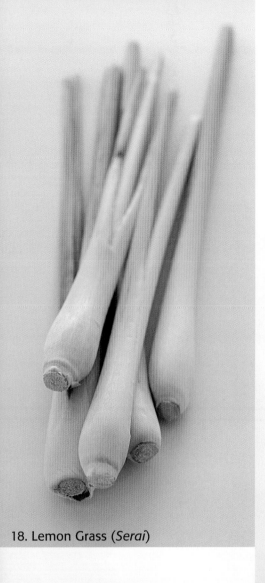

18. Lemon Grass (*Serai*)

20A. Fresh Red Chillies

20B. Fresh Green Chillies

20C. Bird's Eye Chillies (*Cili Padi*)

18A. Lemon Grass Powder

22. Kalamansi Lime (*Limau Kesturi*)

19. Coriander (*Daun Ketumbar*)

21. Shallots (*Bawang Merah*)

23. Fresh Tamarind (*Asam*)

SPICES & HERBS
(continued)

24. Local Chives
(*Ku Chai*)
These long flat green leaves have a subtle onion-like flavour. These are often chopped into short lengths and used in such dishes as Mee Siam.

25. Spring Onions (Scallions)
(*Daun Bawang*)
A young onion with an immature bulb, the spring onion has round hollow leaves and a strong onion-like flavour. Is it usually used as a garnish as well as to season dishes.

Substitute: Western Chives

26. Pink Ginger Buds
(*Bunga Siantan/Bunga Kantan*)
Also known as torch ginger, these beautiful pink buds of the ginger plant are usually finely sliced then added to curries or the Indonesian salad, Rojak. It has a subtle but distinctive flavour.

27. Kaffir Lime Leaf
(*Daun Limau Purut*)
A distinctive leaf because it has two leaves joined end to end. It is usually used whole in curries or finely sliced to release its lovely citrus aroma. Keeps well frozen in a sealed bag.

28. Banana Leaves
(*Daun Pisang*)
Widely used across Asia to wrap savoury food or desserts before cooking to impart a subtle aroma to the dish, while making it aesthetically more pleasing. It is also used as a disposable, organic 'plate'. Wipe thoroughly with a damp cloth before using. Available at wet markets and Asian grocery stores.

29. Screwpine (*Pandan*) Leaves (*Duan Pandan*)
The long, dark, green leaves of this plant are used in both savoury and sweet dishes for its distinct flavour and mild green colour. If used whole for its flavour, rinse or wipe thoroughly, then tie the leaf into a knot to make it easier to cook with. Remove the leaf before serving. To extract the juice, pound or blend with a little water, then strain using muslin cloth or a fine sieve.

26. Pink Ginger Buds (*Bunga Siantan/Bunga Kantan*)

24. Local Chives (*Ku Chai*)

27. Kaffir Lime Leaf (*Daun Limau Purut*)

28. Banana Leaves (*Daun Pisang*)

25. Spring Onions (Scallions)
(*Daun Bawang*)

29. Screwpine (*Pandan*) Leaves (*Duan Pandan*)

COCONUT

PRESERVED FOODSTUFFS

30. Fresh Grated Coconut (*Kelapa*)

Fresh grated coconut is generally squeezed for its cream/milk but is also used in its grated form.
Two types of grated coconut are available at the wet market—(30A) white and (30B) black.
The white variety is skinned before grating while the black variety is grated with the dark coconut skin. Use the white variety for dessert toppings and the black variety for extracting coconut cream/milk.

Fresh grated coconut can be kept in the refrigerator for a few days and in the freezer for weeks. Thaw for about 1 hr before using or add hot water to quicken the process.

Supermarkets are increasingly selling ready-packed freshly squeezed coconut cream/milk so it is sometimes unnecessary to squeeze the cream/milk on your own.

For the health conscious, dilute the coconut milk or substitute completely with skimmed milk or even soy milk.

Substitutes: Pasteurised coconut milk/cream, powdered or desiccated coconut

31. Salted Cabbage (*Kiam Chai*)

It has a crunchy texture and is extremely salty. Rinse or soak for a few minutes before using to remove some, but not all, of the salt. It is usually sold vacuum-sealed or bottled at the wet market, supermarket or Chinese grocery store. Keeps well for months in its brine.

32. Dried Chinese Mushrooms

Frequently used in both Chinese and Peranakan cooking, dried Chinese mushrooms are convenient since they keep well and can be easily rehydrated when required. Soak in hot water to soften then squeeze dry before using. Keeps well for months in a clean airtight container or even better in the freezer.

33. Dried Prawns (Shrimps) (*Udang Kering*)

Also commonly known as *hae bee* (in Hokkien), these salted, dried prawns are a frequently used ingredient in Peranakan cuisine, especially in *rempahs*.

Supermarkets stock them in pre-packed bags, while the wet markets sell them by weight and differentiate them by quality and size. Rinse quickly then shake them dry before use. Keeps well for months in a clean airtight container or even better in the refrigerator or freezer.

34. Dried Whitebait/Anchovies (*Ikan Bilis*)

These are tiny dried fish which are usually deep-fried and eaten as a snack or side dish, or used to enrich stocks. Remove the heads and stomach, if preferred. Quickly rinse then shake them dry before use. Keeps well for months in a clean airtight container or even better in the refrigerator or freezer.

35. Dried Salted Fish

Across Asia, fish is often salted and dried to preserve and intensify its flavour. Small pieces of dried salted fish are often used in soups or stir-fried with vegetables. Keeps well for months in a clean airtight container or even better in the refrigerator or freezer.

36. Dried Cuttlefish (*Sotong Kering*)

Cuttlefish is a relative of the squid. It is often sold in the dried goods section of the wet market or supermarket. It needs to be soaked in warm water for 1–3 hours to soften and to remove the saltiness before it is used. Keeps well for months in a clean airtight container or even better in the refrigerator or freezer.

30A. Fresh Grated Coconut, white (*Kelapa*)

32. Dried Chinese Mushrooms

30B. Fresh Grated Coconut, black (*Kelapa*)

33. Dried Prawns (Shrimps) (*Udang Kering*)

35. Dried Salted Fish

31. Salted Cabbage (*Kiam Chai*)

34. Dried Whitebait/Anchovies (*Ikan Bilis*)

36. Dried Cuttlefish (*Sotong Kering*)

VEGETABLES

37. Long Beans
(*Kacang Panjang*)
These long thin green coloured pods are so named because they grow to be very long. Their soft crunchy texture makes them ideal for salads, curries or stews.

Substitute: French Beans

38. French Beans
Very similar in texture and taste to long beans, French beans are also ideal for salads, curries or stews.

Substitute: Long Beans

39. Local Lettuce
(*Sayur Salad*)
Local lettuce has a curly edge, soft crunchy texture and subtle taste. It is commonly served with spring rolls, used in salads or as a garnish.

Substitute: Romaine or Butter Lettuce.

40. Water Convolvulus
(*Kangkung*)
Known locally as *kangkung*, this is a tasty vegetable that is often cooked at home and at restaurants. Rinse thoroughly before using. Discard the roots and pluck off the leafy parts, retaining some of the stem which adds crunch.

Substitute: Spinach

41. Flowering Cabbage
(*Choy Sum*)
This green leafy vegetable sometimes bears small yellow flowers at its tip. It is often stir-fried or blanched in noodle dishes or soups.

42. Bamboo Shoots
(*Rebung*)
Bamboo shoots are sold fresh or pre-cooked. For fresh bamboo shoots, remove the hard outer layer then simmer until tender. This will take about 1 hour, depending on the size of the piece. Pre-cooked ones are available in cans or vacuum-sealed.

43. Local Turnip/Yam Bean
(*Bang Kuang*)
Also known by its American name, jicama. It has an earthy brown skin and a crisp white-coloured flesh. Always scrub away any soil on its skin before peeling and using. It can be eaten raw in salads because of its natural crunchiness and sweetness but it is commonly stewed since it readily takes on the flavour of the sauce or gravy that it is cooked in.

44. Yam/Taro
(*Keladi*)
This tuber has a rough brown skin and purplish flesh. It is used for both savoury dishes and desserts.

45. Bean Sprouts
(*Tauge*)
With the growing popularity of Asian cuisine, bean sprouts are now available in most supermarkets in major cities. Although most commercially sold bean sprouts have already been prepared, with their heads and tails plucked, some still come with their hard dark green caps and brown roots. Pluck these off by hand, if preferred, then soak in cold water to prevent discolouring.

46. Local/Chinese Cabbage
(*Kobis*)
This round leafy vegetable is commonly used in Chinese cooking. It has a sweet taste and very subtle flavour. It readily takes on the flavour of the dish it is cooked in which makes it ideas for soups, salads and savoury dishes.

37. Long Beans (*Kacang Panjang*)

40. Water Convolvulus (*Kangkung*)

43. Local Turnip/Yam Bean (*Bang Kuang*)

38. French Beans

41. Flowering Cabbage (*Choy Sum*)

44. Yam/Taro (*Keladi*)

39. Local Lettuce (*Sayur Salad*)

42. Bamboo Shoots (*Rebung*)

45. Bean Sprouts (*Tauge*)

46. Local/Chinese Cabbage (*Kobis*)

VEGETABLES
(continued)

47. Chinese Radish
(*Lobak*)
Also known by its Japanese name *daikon*, this long white root is often used in soups and stews. It has a mild sweet flavour and easily soaks up other flavours. It is typically used in soups, braised dishes or pickles. Peel before using.

48. Water Chestnuts
(*Sengkuang Cina*)
Water chestnuts have a distinctive shape. Thoroughly rinse any mud away then peel away its smooth dark brown skin to reveal its white flesh. It has a sweet and crunchy texture and is often used in both savoury and sweet Asian dishes.

49. Canned Button Mushrooms
These are cooked and canned mushrooms which are preserved in brine. They are a versatile ingredient and are often used in Chinese stir-fries. Widely available at wet markets, supermarkets and Chinese grocery stores.

50. Dried Lily Buds
(*Kim Chiam*)
These long, slender, light golden brown buds are aptly named in Chinese as 'golden needles'. They are often added to stews or salads. Some like to knot them before use, although it is not essential. Keeps well in a clean airtight container, in the refrigerator or freezer.

51. Local Eggplant
(*Aubergine/Brinjal*)
Although eggplants come in a variety of shapes and sizes, the local variety is slender, long and light purple in colour. It has white flesh and edible brown seeds. Soak in water after slicing to prevent browning. Used mainly in stir-fries or curries.

52. Okra
(*Ladies' Fingers*)
This long light green coloured vegetable resembles fingers, hence its name. Use whole or sliced in stir-fries or curries.

NOODLES & RICE

53. Dried Glass Noodles
(*Tunghoon*)
These glass noodles become translucent once cooked, hence its name. Made from mung bean flour, it is sometimes also known as mung bean noodles, cellophane noodles or *sohoon*.

It is used in many Asian cuisines, particularly Thai and Vietnamese. Dried glass noodles are available at most supermarkets, wet markets and Chinese grocery stores. Soak them in room temperature water to soften before using.

54. Dried Thin Rice Vermicelli
(*Beehoon*)
Made from rice flour, these dried thin white noodles are usually added to soups or stir-fried. They are available at most supermarkets and in the dried goods section of wet markets. They are also known as rice stick noodles. Soak them in room temperature water before using.

55. White Glutinous Rice
(*Pulut*)
These rounded, opaque white grains of rice are high in starch and become sticky once cooked. They are used in both savoury and sweet dishes. There is also a black glutinous rice (*pulut hitam*) variety which is used for desserts.

56. Basmati Rice
These long, thin and delicate grains of rice go best with South Asian food. It has a slightly nutty flavour and is often cooked with spices, fruits and nuts. Basmati is available at supermarkets, delicatessens/gourmet shops and Indian grocery stores.

47. Chinese Radish (*Lobak*)

53. Dried Glass Noodles (*Tunghoon*)

48. Water Chestnuts (*Sengkuang Cina*)

50. Dried Lily Buds (*Kim Chiam*)

54. Dried Thin Rice Vermicelli (*Beehoon*)

51. Local Eggplant (Aubergine/Brinjal)

55. White Glutinous Rice (*Pulut*)

49. Canned Button Mushrooms

52. Okra (Ladies' Fingers)

56. Basmati Rice

SOY IN VARIOUS FORMS

57. Firm Tofu
(*Taukua*)
Widely used in Peranakan and Asian cuisine, firm tofu is very versatile. It can be boiled, steamed or fried because it retains its shape during cooking, and it takes on the flavour of the dish it is cooked in.

To store freshly made tofu from the wet market, change the water daily and drain excess water before using. For the vacuum-packed tofu from the supermarket, open the packet only when required. Keep refrigerated and discard if not used after 2–3 days or once it smells off.

58. Soft Tofu
(*Tauhu*)
Soft tofu has a soft silky texture and is used in a wide variety of savoury dishes. The very soft variety (*tauhuay*) is used in desserts. It tends to break apart easily so handle with care and do not overcook. Keep refrigerated and discard after 2–3 days if not used or once it smells off. Drain excess water before using.

59. Tofu Puffs
(*Taupok*)
Golden brown on the outside and pale yellow on the inside, these deep-fried square pieces of bean curd are often stuffed or added to salads such as Rojak. Its hollow interior makes it good for stuffing with minced meat or fish.

60. Dried White Tofu Skin
(*Taukee* or *Fong Tauhu*)
These are thin dried sheets of bean curd obtained from the coagulated surface of soy bean milk. The thicker variety is used in savoury dishes such as Chap Chai, while the thinner ones are used in desserts. Soak in cold water to rehydrate before using.

61. Dried White Thin Tofu Skin (*Fupei/Kulit Tauhu*)
This paper-thin sheet is made by steaming soy bean milk until a layer coagulates at the surface. The layer is then removed and hung to dry.

Fupei comes in sheets about 50–70 cm wide and is sold as neatly folded parcels. It has a plastic feel to the touch and is pliable, which makes it easy to wrap meat. Wipe with a damp cloth to clean then cut to the desired size with a knife or pair of scissors.

Fupei is available from the dried goods store in the wet market. It is best to use the Cantonese name, *fupei* (which literally means 'tofu skin' in Cantonese), so as not to confuse it with dried hard brown tofu skin (*fuchok*).

62. Dried Brown Hard Tofu Skin (*Fuchok*)
These sweetened dried pieces of tofu comes in small thick rectangular pieces and are brown in colour. It is has a slightly smoky flavour and is often used in soups and stews, or deep-fried as a garnish.

63. Salted Soy Beans
(*Taucheo*)
These are salted and fermented soy beans with a salty, smoky and strong but pleasant flavour. It is sold whole or minced in bottles. I prefer to buy minced beans since it can be used directly from the bottle. If whole beans are used, pound it first to make a smooth paste. Salted soy beans can keep for years in an unopened bottle. Refrigerate after opening.

64. Fermented Soy Bean Cakes (*Tempe*)
These are pressed and fermented soy bean cakes. Although the presence of mould is a little off-putting, this is what gives it its unique flavour. Commonly used in Malay and Indonesian cuisine, fermented soy bean cakes are not commonly used in Peranakan cooking.

57. Firm Tofu (*Taukua*)

60. Dried White Tofu Skin (*Taukee* or *Fong Tauhu*)

62. Dried Brown Hard Tofu Skin (*Fuchok*)

58. Soft Tofu (*Tauhu*)

61. Dried White Thin Tofu Skin (*Fupei/Kulit Tauhu*)

63. Salted Soy Beans (*Taucheo*)

59. Tofu Puffs (*Taupok*)

64. Fermented Soy Bean Cakes (*Tempe*)

PASTES & SAUCES

65. Chinese Cooking Wine
A little cooking wine goes a long way to enhance the flavour of a dish. Chinese cooking wine is made from glutinous rice fermented with yeast, water and salt. It is available at wet markets, supermarkets and Chinese grocery stores. It is debatable which is the best brand to use, so simply buy the one of the highest quality that you can find.

66. Chinese Rice Vinegar
For the purpose of cooking, a high quality white vinegar would suffice. Made from glutinous rice and water, white rice vinegar is colourless and is therefore best suited for cooking. Avoid using black Chinese vinegar which is mainly used as a seasoning/condiment. If white rice vinegar is not available, Western white vinegar can be used.

67. Sweet Soy Bean Sauce (*Kicap Manis/Cap Kipas Udang*)
This sweet molasses-like sauce is widely used in Indonesian cooking and to a lesser extent in Peranakan cooking. It is made from soy bean extract, wheat flour, caramel, sugar, salt and preservatives. A mixture of 3 parts dark soy sauce, 2 parts molasses and 1 part brown sugar makes a decent substitute.

68. Worcestershire Sauce
A condiment that we have inherited from our colonial past, Lea and Perrins' Worcestershire Sauce has found its way into the mainstay of Singaporean cuisine. Made from vinegar, anchovies, tamarind, onions, garlic, spices, molasses, sugar, salt and other flavouring. It is sold widely in supermarkets.

69. Oyster Sauce
This thick brown sauce is used as an all-purpose seasoning in Chinese cooking either on its own or mixed with other sauces, but it is best used in moderate amounts. There is a wide variety of oyster sauces varying from those made from real oyster extract to those using artificial flavouring. The other ingredients include starch (to thicken the sauce), caramel, sugar and salt.

70. Lingam's Chilli Sauce
This particular brand of sweet chilli sauce is made from red chillies, vinegar, sugar and salt. It is the perfect dipping sauce for various snacks.

71. Black Prawn (Shrimp) Paste (*Haeko*)
This thick black paste is made from prawns, flour, water, sugar and salt, and is sometimes referred to by its Malay name *petis*. It has a thick tar-like consistency, an intense flavour and a pungent smell, which is why it is usually diluted with warm water or other ingredients. It is most associated with dishes such as Rojak and Penang Laksa.

72. Sweet Flour Sauce (*Timcheong*)
Sweet flour sauce is made from sugar, flour and salt, and has a treacle-like consistency. It is served as a dipping sauce for snacks such as Hati Babi or Ngoh Hiang and is a key condiment in Popiah.

73. Plum Jam
It is usually served as a dipping sauce for roasted duck and Chinese cold appetizers. It is made from plums, starch, sugar and water, and is more likely found in the sauce section of the supermarket rather than with the jams and spreads.

74. Tomato Paste
This thick red paste is often used in Western cooking for pasta sauces and stews and has also found its way into Asian cooking. Use it in moderate amounts since it has a strong flavour and is acidic. It is widely available in supermarkets.

75. Prawn (Shrimp) Paste (*Belacan*)
This preserved and fermented paste is synonymous with Peranakan and Southeast Asian cuisine. There is a wide variety in terms of quality, texture (soft or hard) and colour (pink to brown).

My preference is the grey-brown variety from Penang which comes in a small block. It is extremely pungent but has a wonderful flavour. Prawn paste keeps for a long time in an airtight container in the refrigerator. Slice off the required amount, then pound together with *rempah* or toast before using. To toast, wrap the paste in foil to prevent the smell from escaping, then place in the oven or on a dry pan for a few minutes on each side.

76. Preserved Tamarind (*Asam*)
This thick brown paste consists of the pulp and seeds of the tamarind fruit. A key ingredient in Peranakan cuisine, it is used to preserve meat and is appreciated for its strong flavour. To extract the pulp, soak it in a little water, rub the pulp off the seeds with your fingers, then strain. Discard the seeds and use the liquid. Do not store in a metal container since tamarind is highly acidic and therefore corrosive. Instead, place in an earthen pot or plastic bag. It does not require refrigeration and will keep well for months.

Substitutes: Fresh Tamarind or Dried Sour Fruit Slices (*Asam Gelugur*).

65. Chinese Cooking Wine

66. Chinese Rice Vinegar

67. Sweet Soy Bean Sauce (*Kicap Manis/ Cap Kipas Udang*)

68. Worcestershire Sauce

69. Oyster Sauce

70. Lingam's Chilli Sauce

71. Black Prawn (Shrimp) Paste (*Haeko*)

72. Sweet Flour Sauce (*Timcheong*)

73. Plum Jam

74. Tomato Paste

75. Prawn (Shrimp) Paste (*Belacan*)

76. Preserved Tamarind (*Asam*)

OTHERS

79. Corn Flour (Cornstarch)
It is usually used as a thickening agent by mixing first with water or other sauces. It is sometimes also used in batters for a crispy crust.

80. Bicarbonate of Soda
Used in baking and cooking, bicarbonate of soda can also be added when boiling vegetables since it helps to retain the green colour of the vegetables. It is also used as a natural stain and odour remover.

81. Chinese Doughsticks (*You Tiao/You Char Kway*)
These long fritters are deep-fried until light golden brown and crisp. In North East Asia, a typical breakfast would consist of Chinese doughsticks and hot soy bean milk. It is often toasted then eaten whole as a snack, or sliced and added to porridge and desserts. It is an essential ingredient in Rojak.

82. Prawn Crackers (*Keropok*), dried and fried
Traditionally made with minced prawn meat, flour and spices, most commercially available brands nowadays do not contain meat, but just prawn flavouring. It is usually served as a snack, with Lontong or curries. Sun dry or dry in the oven using low heat, then place in hot oil until fully expanded which will only take a few seconds. Drain well then allow to cool before storing in an airtight container.

83. Bitter Nut Crackers (*Emping*), dried and fried
These are made from the bitter nut and are slightly bitter. Prepare in the same way as you would prawn crackers. They are perfect as a snack or eaten with such dishes as Gado Gado. Ready-made ones are sometimes sold with a caramelised sugar coating.

84. Chinese Sausage (*Lap Cheong*)
This is a dried sweet smoky flavoured pork sausage commonly used in Cantonese cuisine. It is also used in the popular Peranakan dish, Popiah. Steam, boil or fry before eating. Chinese sausages are best stored in a cool, dry place or in the freezer.

85. Quail Eggs
These small speckled eggs are used in both sweet and savory Peranakan and Asian dishes. Use as you normally would chicken eggs.

86. Golden or Karo Syrup
Essentially a sugar syrup, this product reflects the influences from Singapore's colonial past.

87. Palm Sugar (*Gula Melaka*)
This unrefined sugar has a rich caramelised flavour. The consistency ranges from a dark brown molasses to a crystallised brown powder. Commonly available in cylindrical tubes, slice or grate the amount you require. It is typically used in Peranakan, Malay and Indonesian desserts and certain savoury dishes.

To make palm sugar syrup, roughly chop then simmer some palm sugar in water together with a knotted screwpine leaf until the sugar has dissolved. Remove and discard the screwpine leaf before serving.

Substitutes: Brown or Muscovado Sugar.

79. Corn Flour (Cornstarch)

82. Prawn Crackers (*Keropok*), dried and fried

85. Quail Eggs

80. Bicarbonate of Soda

83. Bitter Nut Crackers (*Emping*), dried and fried

86. Golden or Karo Syrup

81. Chinese Doughsticks (*You Tiao/You Char Kway*)

84. Chinese Sausage (*Lap Cheong*)

87. Palm Sugar (*Gula Melaka*)

Basic Cooking Techniques

Rempah is the Malay term for spices pounded together.

How to Prepare *Rempah*

1 Prepare all the *rempah* ingredients as listed in the recipe. Soak the dried chillies in hot water to soften (about 15 min). Peel and roughly chop ingredients such as shallots, ginger, turmeric and galangal. Deseed the chillies to make them less spicy, if desired, then roughly chop.

2 Using a mortar and pestle, start by pounding the hardest ingredients first or follow the order laid out in the recipe.

3 Gradually add the remaining ingredients, pounding to a desired consistency each time. The timing as to when each ingredient is to be added and how long pounding is required is a matter of judgment which comes with practice and experience. Pounding for too long or too short a period will result in an uneven consistency or incorrect texture.

4 Continue to pound until the desired texture (course, fine or very fine) is attained. Use as required.

Note:

1 The main difference between pounding by hand and using an electric blender is that pounding by hand gives you better control of the texture, resulting in a better quality *rempah*. The pounding action not only minces the pulp but releases the juices. The blender minces up the ingredients, often too finely, and sometimes water or oil needs to be added for the blender to work smoothly. Although pounding is preferable, for practical purposes, it is acceptable to use a blender.

2 Getting a rhythm to pounding is key since this will result in a more even consistency.

3 Always angle the pestle slightly when pounding so that the ingredients stay in the centre of the mortar. This will result in an even texture.

How to Prepare Coconut Cream/Milk

1 Place the grated coconut into a large bowl then pour water over it. Leave it to soak for a few minutes. The exact amounts of grated coconut and water are listed in the individual recipes.

2 Spoon the pulp into a muslin bag or clean kitchen towel.

3 Over a bowl, twist the bag/towel then squeeze down to extract the coconut cream/milk.

4 Alternatively, squeeze a handful of the pulp with your fingers, over a sieve. This would be considered the first extraction. For a second extraction, repeat the process again. Finally, discard the used grated coconut.

Note:

1 The difference between coconut cream and coconut milk is that coconut cream is obtained from the first extraction using very little water.

2 The first extraction will result in a coconut cream or a thicker, richer coconut milk, depending on the amount of water used. The second extraction will result in a more diluted coconut milk.

3 When boiling coconut milk, stir continuously and do not overboil, or it will *pecah minyak* (split). This means it will curdle and the coconut oil will separate.

4 A little salt is sometimes added to grated coconut or coconut cream/milk to enhance its flavour and preserve it.

5 Grated coconut and dishes cooked using coconut milk will spoil easily, so keep them refrigerated. Discard fresh grated coconut after 1–2 days in the refrigerator or keep frozen.

How to Prepare Tamarind Marinade

1 In a bowl, combine the tamarind and water according to the amount listed in the recipe.

2 Using your fingers, rub the tamarind pulp off the seeds.

3 Strain the mixture through a sieve. Discard the seeds. Use as required.

Basic Kitchen Equipment

Perforated Ladle

- Ideal for scooping up and draining food.

'Cooking' Chopsticks

- Compared to ordinary table chopsticks, these chopsticks are thicker and longer. They are perfect for frying and tossing noodles.

Rounded Ladle

- Rounded ladles are ideal for scooping out and serving anything with a lot of liquid.
- More experienced and traditional chefs also use it to measure quantities of liquid such as oil, water or stock. One ladleful is equivalent to about 5 tbsp.

Wok Ladle

- The wok ladle is one of the most commonly used instruments in Asian cooking. It is used for stir-frying, tossing, lifting and scooping.
- The slightly rounded edge of the wok ladle fits the contours of the wok perfectly.

Mortar and Pestle *(Batu Lesung)*

- This mortar and pestle pictured here is the same one that was illustrated in the original edition of *Mrs Lee's Cookbook*. It has been in my family for at least 40 years and was used by my grandmother.
- To season a mortar and pestle, use it to pound some sand. Discard the sand then pound some vegetable remnants. Discard the pounded vegetable remnants and repeat the process twice. Finally, pound some raw rice until it is fine. Discard the rice and repeat this process until the mortar and pestle are smooth and the pounded rice is white in colour.

Wok *(Kuali)*

- There are various types of woks: iron, steel and non-stick. Iron woks are preferable since they can last for decades and get better with age. Woks are extremely versatile. They can be used for frying, steaming, boiling, braising and toasting.

- A well-seasoned wok will enhance the taste of the food cooked in it. If well taken care of, a wok can be passed down generations like a family heirloom. This one pictured here is at least 40 years old, if not more. It is the wok that my grandmother cooked with. It continues to be used in my home today and was used to cook the dishes in this cookbook.

- Iron woks need to be seasoned before use. The traditional method my grandmother used was to fry the pulp of a grated coconut until dry. Discard the pulp then quickly rinse the wok. Next, halve an onion and rub it on the inner surface of the wok. Roughly chop the onion, then heat 2 tbsp of oil in the wok and fry the chopped onion. Discard the onion and oil. Wipe it clean then coat it with a layer of clean oil. Repeat this process if necessary.

- A common way to remove burnt food is by soaking the wok in water until the residue comes off. If necessary, scrub the burnt area, wash with soap, rinse, dry then coat with a layer of clean oil.

- Avoid scrubbing the wok with anything abrasive, unless removing burnt food, and always coat it with a layer of clean oil after use to prevent rusting.

- Enamel and non-stick woks do not require seasoning and are generally easier to cook with, but be careful not to scratch the surface. Avoid using metal ladles and discard the wok once the surface is scratched.

Steamer

- Steamers offer an efficient and healthy way of cooking. While blanching or boiling food, particularly vegetables, causes nutrients and flavours to be lost, this is less so with steaming. I use the steamer when there are a number of ingredients I need to cook separately, for example when preparing Gado Gado. The top section can be used to steam vegetables, while the bottom section can be used to boil eggs.
- I use this particular enamel steamer for steaming Nasi Lemak because the small holes in the steamer basket prevents the rice from falling through.

Chinese Cleaver

- The Chinese cleaver is extremely versatile. It can be used for slicing, crushing, mincing, tenderising and scrapping. It is my favourite piece of kitchen equipment because, like the wok, it is simple in its construct but has a wide range of uses. With practice and some skill, it can be used to deftly slice fine sheets of tofu or cut a whole chicken into pieces in a matter of seconds.
- **To slice:** hold the cleaver firmly in one hand. With the other hand, place it firmly on the ingredient then curl your fingers. Lean the flat side of the cleaver against your knuckles and proceed to slice using an upward and downward motion.
- **To crush:** hold the cleaver firmly in one hand. Lay the flat end of the cleaver onto the ingredient then press firmly with the other hand. Alternatively, smash the blade flat against the ingredient. This is the easiest way to remove the skin off of a clove of garlic or bruise a piece of lemon grass or turmeric.
- **To mince:** hold the cleaver firmly in one hand and repeatedly chop across a piece of meat/vegetable then fold it over by lifting it with the blade. This is perfect for mincing tofu, fish or pork. Garlic/shallots can also be roughly or finely minced using this same method.
- **To tenderise:** hold the cleaver firmly in one hand with the blunt edge of the blade facing down. Repeatedly chop across a piece of meat, then flip the piece of meat over by lifting it with the blade. Repeat until the meat is of the desired texture.
- **To scrape:** hold the cleaver firmly in one hand then run the sharp blade across a piece of meat/vegetable. This is useful for removing excess fat off a piece of meat.

Roti Jala Maker (*Acuan Roti Jala*)

- A specially designed cup with 4–5 funnels, traditionally made of brass but commonly made of plastic today. It is ideal but not essential for making Roti Jala, a traditional lacy pancake.

Noodle Strainer

- Perfect for lifting noodles or draining food from a wok.

Useful Contacts

Shermay's Cooking School Pte Ltd

Chip Bee Gardens, Blk 43 Jalan Merah Saga #03-64

Singapore 278115

tel: +65 6479 8442   fax: +65 6479 8414

email: shermaycs@yahoo.com.sg

website: www.shermay.com

Raffles Hotel, Tiffin Room

1 Beach Road, Singapore 189673

tel: +65 6337 1886   fax: +65 6339 7650

email: raffles@raffles.com

webste: www.raffleshotel.com

Sia Huat Pte Ltd

7, 9 & 11 Temple Street, Singapore 058559

tel: +65 6223 1732   fax: +65 6224 2896

email: enquiry@siahuat.com.sg

website: www.siahuat.com.sg

Opening hours:

Monday to Friday: 8:30 am to 6:30 pm

Saturday: 8:30 am to 5:30 pm

Closed on Sunday and public holidays

The Butcher

Chip Bee Gardens, Blk 44 Jalan Merah Saga #01-50

Singapore 276116

tel: +65 6472 0073   fax: +65 6472 0078

website: www.thebutcher.com.sg

Opening hours:

Monday to Friday: 10 am to 8 pm

Saturday and Sunday: 10 am to 6 pm

Weights and Measures

Quantities for this book are given in Metric and American (spoon and cup) measures. Standard spoon and cup measurements used are: 1 teaspoon = 5 ml, 1 tablespoon = 15 ml, 1 cup = 250 ml. All measures are level unless otherwise stated.

LIQUID AND VOLUME MEASURES

Metric	Imperial	American
5 ml	$^1/_6$ fl oz	1 teaspoon
10 ml	$^1/_3$ fl oz	1 dessertspoon
15 ml	$^1/_2$ fl oz	1 tablespoon
60 ml	2 fl oz	$^1/_4$ cup (4 tablespoons)
85 ml	$2^1/_2$ fl oz	$^1/_3$ cup
90 ml	3 fl oz	$^3/_8$ cup (6 tablespoons)
125 ml	4 fl oz	$^1/_2$ cup
180 ml	6 fl oz	$^3/_4$ cup
250 ml	8 fl oz	1 cup
300 ml	10 fl oz ($^1/_2$ pint)	$1^1/_4$ cups
375 ml	12 fl oz	$1^1/_2$ cups
435 ml	14 fl oz	$1^3/_4$ cups
500 ml	16 fl oz	2 cups
625 ml	20 fl oz (1 pint)	$2^1/_2$ cups
750 ml	24 fl oz ($1^1/_5$ pints)	3 cups
1 litre	32 fl oz ($1^3/_5$ pints)	4 cups
1.25 litres	40 fl oz (2 pints)	5 cups
1.5 litres	48 fl oz ($2^2/_5$ pints)	6 cups
2.5 litres	80 fl oz (4 pints)	10 cups

OVEN TEMPERATURE

	°C	°F	Gas Regulo
Very slow	120	250	1
Slow	150	300	2
Moderately slow	160	325	3
Moderate	180	350	4
Moderately hot	190/200	370/400	5/6
Hot	210/220	410/440	6/7
Very hot	230	450	8
Super hot	250/290	475/550	9/10

DRY MEASURES

Metric	Imperial
30 grams	1 ounce
45 grams	$1^1/_2$ ounces
55 grams	2 ounces
70 grams	$2^1/_2$ ounces
85 grams	3 ounces
100 grams	$3^1/_2$ ounces
110 grams	4 ounces
125 grams	$4^1/_2$ ounces
140 grams	5 ounces
280 grams	10 ounces
450 grams	16 ounces (1 pound)
500 grams	1 pound, $1^1/_2$ ounces
700 grams	$1^1/_2$ pounds
800 grams	$1^3/_4$ pounds
1 kilogram	2 pounds, 3 ounces
1.5 kilograms	3 pounds, $4^1/_2$ ounces
2 kilograms	4 pounds, 6 ounces

LENGTH

Metric	Imperial
0.5 cm	$^1/_4$ inch
1 cm	$^1/_2$ inch
1.5 cm	$^3/_4$ inch
2.5 cm	1 inch

OTHER MEASURES

1 thumb size knob = 5 cm

ABBREVIATION

tsp	teaspoon
tbsp	tablespoon
g	gram
kg	kilogram
ml	millilitre
l	litre
min	minute(s)
hr	hour(s)